QlikView for Developers Cookbook

Discover the strategies needed to tackle the most challenging tasks facing the QlikView developer

Stephen Redmond

PUBLISHING

BIRMINGHAM - MUMBAI

QlikView for Developers Cookbook

First published: June 2013

Production Reference: 1170613

Published by Packt Publishing Ltd.
Livery Place
35 Livery Street
Birmingham B3 2PB, UK.

ISBN 978-1-78217-973-3

www.packtpub.com

Cover Image by Stephen Redmond (stephen.c.redmond@gmail.com)

Credits

Author

Stephen Redmond

Reviewers

Steve Dark

Ralf Becher

Miguel Ángel García

Barry Harmsen

Acquisition Editor

Usha Iyer

Lead Technical Editors

Rukmini Iyer

Neeshma Ramakrishnan

Technical Editors

Jalasha D'costa

Saumya Kunder

Lubna Shaikh

Amit Ramadas

Project Coordinator

Apeksha Chitnis

Proofreader

Amy Guest

Indexer

Monica Ajmera Mehta

Production Coordinator

Manu Joseph

Cover Work

Manu Joseph

Foreword

"If you can't explain it simply, you do not understand it well enough."

This quote, often attributed to Albert Einstein, very nicely sums up my thoughts on how to best test and improve your (QlikView) skills and knowledge. Starting out as a hands-on practitioner, this lead to me teaching QlikView and writing a blog about it, and culminated in 2012 when Miguel García and I wrote the book *QlikView 11 for Developers*.

When we finished writing the first draft of the book back in June 2012, our editor asked us to recommend people for technical review. Stephen Redmond was one of the first persons to come to my mind. Anyone who has read his blog or interacted with him can see that he knows QlikView. More importantly though, as I know from experience, he also has no problem voicing a strong opinion. Since we intended for *QlikView 11 for Developers* to compete on quality and depth of subject, Stephen was an ideal technical reviewer to challenge us. Along with that of the other technical reviewers, Stephen's expert feedback helped ensure that our book achieved the quality and depth that we strived for.

After being published in November 2012, *QlikView 11 for Developers* quickly became the best rated and best-selling book on QlikView, and has continued to do very well. It has helped novices take their first steps in QlikView, as well as help more experienced developers prepare for their certifications.

Given the success of *QlikView 11 for Developers*, you can imagine that I was initially skeptical when I learned that our publisher wanted to release another book about QlikView. Why would you need another book?

I was reassured, however, when I learned that Stephen would be taking on the job. Not only because his involvement in our book would ensure minimal overlap between the two titles, but also because I was (and am) confident that he would deliver quality material that appeals to anyone who is looking to further enhance his or her QlikView skills and knowledge. The man who brought us the "Redmond Debt Profile Chart" was bound to have many more interesting and innovative recipes up his sleeve.

As a technical reviewer for this book, I got a first-hand look at the materials Stephen was producing and I can tell you that this is quite a different book that will be a valuable addition to your library. Stephen's cookbook allows for casual, bite-sized reads by offering self-contained recipes. It is as if you've just discovered a completely new QlikView blog with dozens of tips and tricks. The recipes will take you from simple-but-effective tricks to sophisticated solutions. Even I have found a few recipes that I cannot wait to serve my clients. Best of all, they are all explained in a simple, straightforward manner, demonstrating that Stephen absolutely understands QlikView very well.

Barry Harmsen

Independent Business Intelligence Consultant, Co-author of *QlikView 11 for Developers*, and blogger at `www.qlikfix.com`.

About the Author

Stephen Redmond is CTO of CapricornVentis Limited (`http://www.capventis.com`), a QlikView Elite Partner. He is the author of several books, including the very popular DevLogix series for SalesLogix developers.

In 2006, after working for many years with CRM systems, reporting and analysis solutions, and data integration, Stephen started working with QlikView. Since then, CapricornVentis have become QlikView's top partner in the UK and the Ireland territory and, with Stephen at the head of the team, have implemented QlikView in a wide variety of enterprises and large business customers across a wide range of sectors from public sector to financial services to large retailers.

Stephen regularly contributes to online forums, including the Qlik Community. His QlikView blog is at `http://qliktips.blogspot.com`, and you can follow him on Twitter (`@stephencredmond`), where he tweets about QlikView, BI, data visualization, and technology in general.

I would like to thank my family for their ongoing support. None of what I do would be possible with them.

A big shout out to my colleagues at CapricornVentis, who are a great team to work with.

A special thanks to all of the customers that I have worked with implementing QlikView. It is your business issues that have inspired me to create the solutions that occupy these pages.

About the Reviewers

For 10 years, **Steve Dark** was a SQL Server / MS ASP developer building web based reporting solutions, until he was shown a demo of QlikView. Soon after this revelation, Steve left his previous employer to set up Quick Intelligence – a consultancy focusing entirely on QlikView and delivering business intelligence solutions. Preferring to stay at the coal face, Steve spends the majority of his time with clients building QlikView applications, managing QlikView deployments, and running projects.

He will never tire of showing QlikView to new users and seeing that "jaw drop moment".

Steve is active on QlikCommunity and other social media sites sharing his enthusiasm for QlikView and assisting other users. Through his blog, he shares tutorials, examples, and insights about QlikView (read it at `http://www.quickintelligence.co.uk/`).

Steve was also the technical reviewer of *QlikView 11 For Developers* by *Barry Harmsen* and *Miguel García*, *Packt Publishing*.

> I would like to thank Stephen for putting this book together, and for his excellent QlikTips blog.

Ralf Becher has worked as an IT system architect and as an IT consultant since 1989, in the areas of banking, insurance, logistics, automotive, and retail. He founded TIQ Solutions in 2004 with his partners.

The Leipzig company specializes in modern, quality-assured data management; since 2004, it has been helping its customers process, evaluate, and maintain the quality of company data, helping them introduce, implement, and improve complex solutions in the fields of data architecture, data integration, data migration, master data management, metadata management, data warehousing, and business intelligence.

Ralf is an internationally recognized QlikView expert with a strong position in the QlikCommunity. He started working with QlikView in 2006 and has contributed QlikView add-on solutions for data quality and data integration, especially for connectivity in the Java and Big Data realm. He runs his QlikView data integration blog at http://tiqview.tumblr.com/.

Miguel Ángel García is a Business Intelligence Consultant and QlikView Solutions Architect from Monterrey, Mexico. Having worked throughout many successful QlikView implementations, from its inception through implementation, and performed across a wide variety of roles on each project, his experience and skills range from applications development and design, to presales, technical architecture, system administration, as well as functional analysis and overall project execution.

He currently holds the QlikView Designer, QlikView Developer, and QlikView System Administrator Certifications.

He is the co-author of the *QlikView 11 for Developers* book, published in November 2012 by *Packt Publishing*.

Barry Harmsen is an independent Business Intelligence Consultant based in the Netherlands. Originally from a background of traditional business intelligence, data warehousing, and performance management, in 2008, he made the shift to QlikView and a more user-centric form of business intelligence.

Since switching over to QlikView, Barry has completed many successful implementations in many different industries, from financial services to telecoms, and from manufacturing to healthcare. Barry's QlikView experience covers a wide variety of roles and subjects; requirements analysis, design, development, architecture, infrastructure, system administration, integration, project management, and training.

In 2012, Barry co-authored the book *QlikView 11 for Developers*. This book has quickly become the must-have book within the QlikView community. Barry writes a QlikView blog at QlikFix.com and can be followed on Twitter at @meneerharmsen.

www.PacktPub.com

Support files, eBooks, discount offers and more

You might want to visit www.PacktPub.com for support files and downloads related to your book.

Did you know that Packt offers eBook versions of every book published, with PDF and ePub files available? You can upgrade to the eBook version at www.PacktPub.com and as a print book customer, you are entitled to a discount on the eBook copy. Get in touch with us at service@packtpub.com for more details.

At www.PacktPub.com, you can also read a collection of free technical articles, sign up for a range of free newsletters and receive exclusive discounts and offers on Packt books and eBooks.

http://PacktLib.PacktPub.com

Do you need instant solutions to your IT questions? PacktLib is Packt's online digital book library. Here, you can access, read and search across Packt's entire library of books.

Why Subscribe?

- ► Fully searchable across every book published by Packt
- ► Copy and paste, print and bookmark content
- ► On demand and accessible via web browser

Free Access for Packt account holders

If you have an account with Packt at www.PacktPub.com, you can use this to access PacktLib today and view nine entirely free books. Simply use your login credentials for immediate access.

Instant Updates on New Packt Books

Get notified! Find out when new books are published by following @PacktEnterprise on Twitter, or the *Packt Enterprise* Facebook page.

Table of Contents

Preface

There is no substitute for experience.

QlikView is a great technology for delivering information and, unusually for a "BI" product, is quite easy to get up and running with simple data sets – they even have a wizard that can get you up and running off an Excel file without having to do any scripting. If you need to bring in more complex data sets, you need to get into the script. Even then, there are some wizards available that will write most of the script for you.

To start your learning process, there are free resources available from `http://www.qlikview.com/training`. There is a very active community forum on `http://community.qlikview.com`, where you can ask questions and get answers. There is a really excellent book that teaches you how to develop in QlikView, *QlikView 11 for Developers* by *Barry Harmsen* and *Mike García* (`http://www.packtpub.com/qlikview-11-developers/book`). Then, if you still need it after all that, you can attend official QlikView classroom training. But, there is no substitute for experience.

At CapricornVentis, we don't just train and leave. We schedule time with the trainees to sit with them, one-on-one, and work on their data, to give them the benefit of our experience, to answer all of those, "How do I do that" questions. We do this because we understand that training isn't enough. It is a great start, but there is no substitute for experience.

And this, I hope, is what this book is—the benefit of my experience.

I have been working with QlikView since 2006. As well as working at the coalface, delivering great solutions, I have also been delivering QlikView training for most of that time. I was one of the first two people in the world (neither of us is sure who was first!) to be certified when QlikView brought out their first developer certification on Version 8. I was one of the earliest certified on designer for Version 8. I have since been recertified on every version up to the latest certifications on Version 11. I have been writing about QlikView on my blog, `http://qliktips.blogspot.com`, since 2009. I have quite a lot of experience with QlikView. And there is no substitute for experience.

What this book covers

Chapter 1, Charts, will look at advanced charting topics such as creating custom pop ups, box charts, bullet charts, and the Redmond chart. We also look at some tips and tricks to create great visualizations.

Chapter 2, Layout, will look at how to modify some of the default layout options and colors, as well as discussing better ways to layout objects.

Chapter 3, Set Analysis, shows some advanced examples of using set analysis in different scenarios.

Chapter 4, Advanced Aggregations, looks at parameters such as TOTAL and functions such as AGGR and the Range functions that allow us to perform vertical calculations.

Chapter 5, Advanced Coding, uses VBScript coding to extract data from QlikView, generate reports, create QlikView objects, and enhance QlikView functionality.

Chapter 6, Data Modeling, covers the area of key tables and link tables, an area that can be confused with new QlikView developers.

Chapter 7, Extensions, introduces the ability to create new visualizations with web technologies and integrate them into QlikView documents.

Chapter 8, Useful Functions, gives you examples of using some of QlikView's very useful functions in different scenarios.

Chapter 9, Script, takes your QlikView scripting a step beyond training. Includes discussion on creating flags, exists and keep, default formats, partial loads, peek and previous, and interval match.

Chapter 10, Improving Performance, shows how to improve the performance of a QlikView data model. Discusses strategies such as reducing data sizes and optimizing expressions. Also, when and when not to denormalize for performance.

Chapter 11, Security, goes through some of the most common issues around section access security in QlikView.

What you need for this book

You need a copy of QlikView Desktop, which you can download for free from `http://www.qlikview.com/download`. After that, you shouldn't need anything else.

To demonstrate the different techniques and functions, I will usually get you to load a table of data. We do this using the `INLINE` function. For example:

```
Load * Inline [
  Field1, Field2
  Value1, Value2
  Value3, Value4
];
```

This will load a table with two fields (`Field1` and `Field2`) and two rows of data.

Most of the time, this type of table is enough for what we need to do. In the few examples, where I need you to use more data than that, we will use publicly available data sources.

Who this book is for

This book is for anyone who has loaded data in QlikView, created a few charts, and then asked the question, "How do I?" If you have either attended QlikView Developer training or have taught yourself QlikView from books or online sources, this book is meant for you. You might be working for a QlikView customer, partner, or even QlikView themselves (or want to) and want to improve your QlikView skills.

Conventions

In this book, you will find a number of styles of text that distinguish between different kinds of information. Here are some examples of these styles, and an explanation of their meaning.

Code words in text are shown as follows: "We do this using the `INLINE` function."

A block of code is set as follows:

```
Sales:
Load * INLINE [

  Country, Sales
  USA, 1000
  UK, 940
  Japan, 543
];
```

When we wish to draw your attention to a particular part of a code block, the relevant lines or items are set in bold:

```
Sales:
Load * INLINE [

   Country, Sales
   USA, 1000
   UK, 940
   Japan, 543
];
```

Any command-line input or output is written as follows:

```
C:\Program Files\QlikView\qv.exe
```

New terms and **important words** are shown in bold. Words that you see on the screen, in menus or dialog boxes for example, appear in the text like this: "Click on the **Extension Objects** menu."

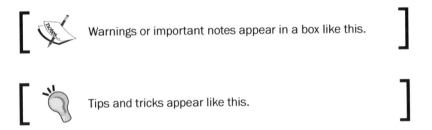

Warnings or important notes appear in a box like this.

Tips and tricks appear like this.

Reader feedback

Feedback from our readers is always welcome. Let us know what you think about this book—what you liked or may have disliked. Reader feedback is important for us to develop titles that you really get the most out of.

To send us general feedback, simply send an e-mail to feedback@packtpub.com, and mention the book title via the subject of your message.

If there is a topic that you have expertise in and you are interested in either writing or contributing to a book, see our author guide on www.packtpub.com/authors.

Customer support

Now that you are the proud owner of a Packt book, we have a number of things to help you to get the most from your purchase.

Downloading the example code

You can download the example code files for all Packt books you have purchased from your account at `http://www.packtpub.com`. If you purchased this book elsewhere, you can visit `http://www.packtpub.com/support` and register to have the files e-mailed directly to you.

Errata

Although we have taken every care to ensure the accuracy of our content, mistakes do happen. If you find a mistake in one of our books—maybe a mistake in the text or the code—we would be grateful if you would report this to us. By doing so, you can save other readers from frustration and help us improve subsequent versions of this book. If you find any errata, please report them by visiting `http://www.packtpub.com/submit-errata`, selecting your book, clicking on the **errata submission form** link, and entering the details of your errata. Once your errata are verified, your submission will be accepted and the errata will be uploaded on our website, or added to any list of existing errata, under the Errata section of that title. Any existing errata can be viewed by selecting your title from `http://www.packtpub.com/support`.

Piracy

Piracy of copyright material on the Internet is an ongoing problem across all media. At Packt, we take the protection of our copyright and licenses very seriously. If you come across any illegal copies of our works, in any form, on the Internet, please provide us with the location address or website name immediately so that we can pursue a remedy.

Please contact us at `copyright@packtpub.com` with a link to the suspected pirated material.

We appreciate your help in protecting our authors, and our ability to bring you valuable content.

Questions

You can contact us at `questions@packtpub.com` if you are having a problem with any aspect of the book, and we will do our best to address it.

1
Charts

In this chapter, we will cover:

- ▸ Creating custom pop-up labels in a bar chart
- ▸ Creating a box plot chart for a simple data set
- ▸ Using the wizard to create a box plot chart
- ▸ Creating a "Stephen Few" bullet chart
- ▸ Creating a modified bullet chart in a straight table
- ▸ Creating a bar chart in a straight table
- ▸ Creating a Redmond Aged Debt Profile chart
- ▸ Creating a waterfall chart
- ▸ Replacing the legend in a line chart with labels on each line
- ▸ Creating a secondary dimension in a bar chart
- ▸ Creating a line chart with variable width lines
- ▸ Brushing parallel coordinates
- ▸ Using redundant encoding with a scatter chart
- ▸ Staggering labels in a pie chart
- ▸ Creating dynamic ad hoc analysis in QlikView

Introduction

Charts are the most important area of QlikView because they are the main method of information delivery, and QlikView is all about information delivery.

There are a few terms that I want to just define before we get cracking, just to make sure you know what I am talking about.

The basis of every chart is some kind of calculation—you add up some numbers or you count something. In QlikView, these calculations are called **expressions**. Every chart should have at least one expression. In fact, some charts require more than one expression.

Most of the time, the expression value that is calculated is not presented in isolation. The calculation is normally made for each of the values in a category. This category is generally the values within a field of data, for example, country or month, in the QlikView data model, but it could be a more complex calculated value. Either way, in QlikView charts, this category is called a **dimension**. Some charts, such as a gauge, would normally never have any dimension. Other charts, such as a pivot table, will often have more than one dimension.

Many simple charts will have just one dimension and one expression. For historical and mathematical reasons, the dimension is sometimes called the **X-Axis** and the expression is sometimes called the **Y-Axis** and you may see these terms used in QlikView.

Creating custom pop-up labels on a bar chart

The default pop up for a QlikView bar chart is useful but is not always exactly what you want.

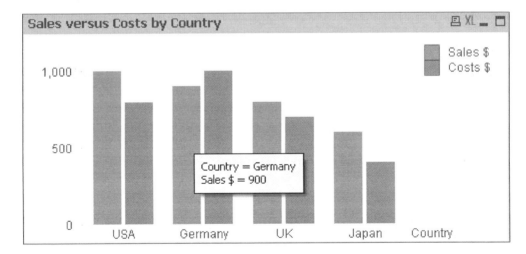

The format is as follows:

Dimension name = value

Expression label = value

Now, we may not like this pop up and wish to display the values differently or add different formats. We may even want to include additional information.

In the preceding example, the pop up shows the value of Sales $ for Germany. If I want to see the value of the Costs $, I need to hover over the Costs $ bar. And what if I wanted to see Margin $ or Margin %?

Getting ready

Create a new QlikView document and save it to a folder. Edit the script (*Ctrl + E* or the **File** menu – **Edit Script**).

Enter the following script:

```
LOAD * INLINE [
    Country, Sales, Costs
    USA, 1000, 800
    UK, 800, 700
    Germany, 900, 1000
    Japan, 600, 400
];
```

Downloading the example code

You can download the example code files for all Packt books you have purchased from your account at `http://www.packtpub.com`. If you purchased this book elsewhere, you can visit `http://www.packtpub.com/support` and register to have the files e-mailed directly to you.

How to do it...

Use the following steps to create a new bar chart and add custom labels:

1. Create a new bar chart with the following characteristics:

Dimension	Country
Expression 1	Sum(Sales)
Expression 2	Sum(Costs)

2. Click on **Finish**.

3. You should see a bar chart with two bars for each country. Confirm that the pop up on each bar displays as expected.

4. Open the chart properties.

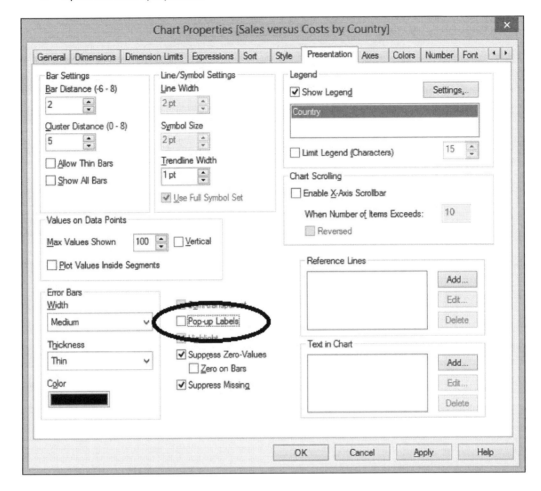

5. Click on the **Presentation** tab and deselect the **Pop-up Labels** checkbox. Click on **OK** and note that there are no longer any pop-up labels appearing.

6. Edit the properties again and click on the **Expressions** tab. Click on the **Add...** button and enter the following expression:

```
='Sales : ' & Num(Sum(Sales), '#,##0')
```

7. Click on **OK**.

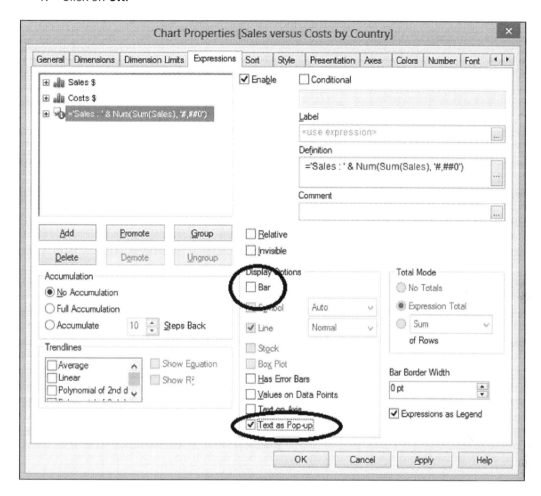

8. Deselect the **Bar** option for this expression and turn on the **Text as Pop-up** option. Click on **OK**.

> Note that the new custom pop up is now active and displays the sales value whether you hover over the **Sales $** or **Costs $** bar.

9. Edit the properties again and edit the pop-up expression as follows:

```
= Country & chr(10)
& 'Sales : ' & Num(Sum(Sales), '$(MoneyFormat)') & chr(10)
& 'Costs : ' & Num(Sum(Costs), '$(MoneyFormat)') & chr(10)
& 'Margin : ' & Num(Sum(Sales)-Sum(Costs), '$(MoneyFormat)')
& chr(10) & 'Margin % : '
& Num(1-(Sum(Costs)/Sum(Sales)), '0.0%')
```

10. Click on **OK** on the expression editor and then click on **OK** to close the properties.

11. Check that the custom pop up is displayed.

How it works...

By turning off the **Bar** option for the expression, QlikView will not try and evaluate the expression as a value and will not try to render a bar for it. By turning on the **Text as Pop-up** option, we tell QlikView to calculate the text of the expression and display it in the pop up.

We also had to turn off the default pop-up option in the **Presentation** tab or else it would display both (which might be what you want, have a play with it).

The chr function is useful to know about adding, so called, non-printable characters into your output. chr(10) is a line feed that moves the text onto the next line.

 Note that we have used a variable here for the format string. MoneyFormat is one of the standard QlikView variables that are generated in the script when you first open the script editor.

There's more...

The cool thing about this is that you can use it everywhere! It works in a lot of different charts and is a great way of giving users additional information about the data that they are looking at.

Creating a box plot chart for a simple data set

Box plot charts, or box and whisker charts, are often used for displaying statistical mean and quartile information.

This can be useful for seeing how a value ranges across categories by visualizing the median, the twenty-fifth and seventy-fifth percentile, and the outlying values.

With a simple data set, it is easier to create the chart manually than using the wizard that QlikView provides—although there is a slightly strange sequence of actions to go through a "funny"—that you need to know about.

Getting ready

Load the following script:

```
LOAD * INLINE [
    Country, Value
    USA, 12
    USA, 14.5
    USA, 6.6
    USA, 4.5
    USA, 7.8
    USA, 9.4
    UK, 11.3
    UK, 10.1
    UK, 3.2
    UK, 5.6
    UK, 3.9
    UK, 6.9
];
```

How to do it...

There is a "funny" in here because you have to tell the chart properties that you are using a box plot, then click on **OK** and then go back in and edit the properties. Here's how you do it:

1. Create a new combo chart. Select **Country** as the dimension.

2. When the expression editor pops up, just enter 0 as the expression. It doesn't really matter what you enter, you just need to enter something.

3. Deselect **Bar** and select **Box Plot**. At this stage, just click on **Finish**. Your chart will come up with **No Data to Display**—this is not a problem.

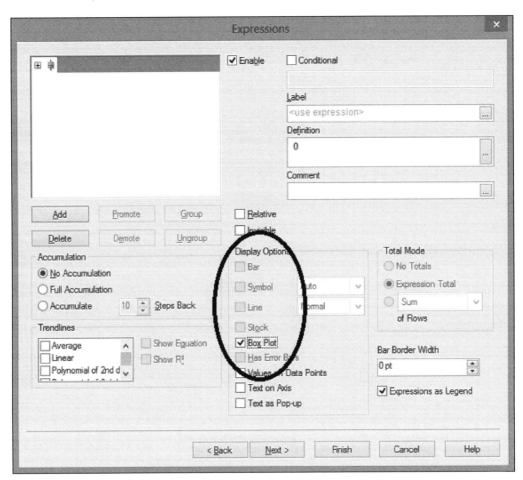

4. When you go back into editing the expression properties, you will find five new subexpressions. Enter the following expressions for each of them:

Box Plot Top	Fractile(Value, .75)
Box Plot Bottom	Fractile(Value, .25)
Box Plot Middle	Fractile(Value, .5)
Box Plot Upper Whisker	Max(Value)
Box Plot Lower Whisker	Min(Value)

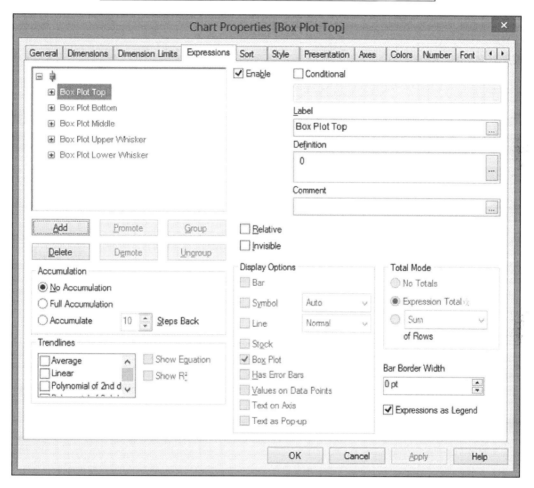

5. Add two new expressions:

   ```
   Max(Value)
   Min(Value)
   ```

6. For the two new expressions, deselect the **Line** option (or **Bar** if it is selected) and select the **Symbol** option. Select **Circles** from the **Symbol** drop-down menu:

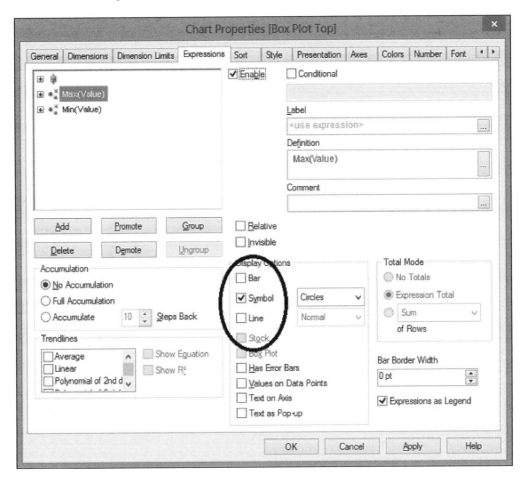

7. On the **Presentation** tab, turn off **Show Legend**. Set the **Symbol Size** option to 3 pt:

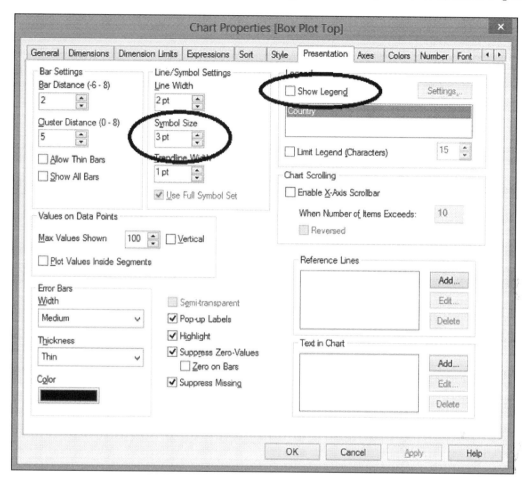

8. Check that the box plot looks like the following screenshot:

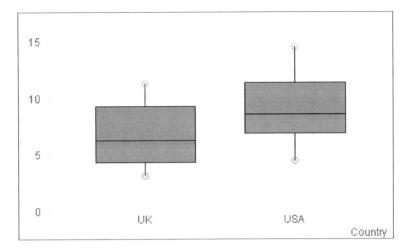

How it works...

The five separate values define the different portions of the box plot:

Top	The top of the box
Bottom	The bottom of the box
Middle	The median value, the line in the box
Upper Whisker	The upper outlier value
Lower Whisker	The lower outlier value

There's more...

This recipe is for when you have a simple set of data and you are looking for the statistics across all of the data.

In QlikView, we can have much more control of the values in the box plot, especially where we want to look at averages and percentiles of aggregated data.

As well as box plots, within the combo chart settings there is also a **Stock** option, which allows us to specify the minimum, the maximum as well as an open and close value.

See also

▸ The *Using the wizard to create a box plot chart* recipe

Using the wizard to create a box plot chart

With a simple data set, we want to see the median (or mean) values and different percentile values across the whole data set. But quite often, we want to look for a particular dimension (for example, Month), at the median and percentiles of the totals for another dimension (for example, Country). So, rather than the median for the individual values (say Sales), which could be quite small or quite large, we want to see the median for the total value by the second dimension.

We can create this manually, but this can be achieved quickly using the Box Plot Wizard.

Getting ready

Load the following script:

```
LOAD * INLINE [
    Country, Value, Month
    USA, 12, 2013-01-01
    USA, 14.5, 2013-01-01
    USA, 6.6, 2013-02-01
    USA, 4.5, 2013-02-01
    USA, 7.8, 2013-03-01
    USA, 9.4, 2013-03-01
    UK, 11.3, 2013-01-01
    UK, 10.1, 2013-01-01
    UK, 3.2, 2013-02-01
    UK, 5.6, 2013-02-01
    UK, 3.9, 2013-03-01
    UK, 6.9, 2013-03-01
];
```

How to do it...

Use the following steps to create a box plot using the wizard:

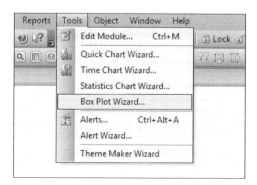

1. From the **Tools** menu, select **Box Plot Wizard....**

2. On the introductory page, click on **Next**:

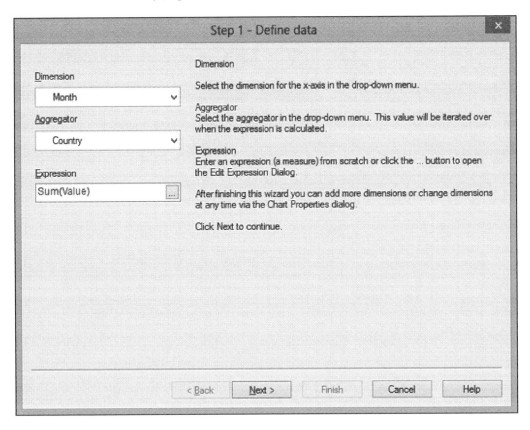

3. Select the following values:

Dimension	Month
Aggregator	Country
Expression	Sum(Value)

4. Click on **Next**.

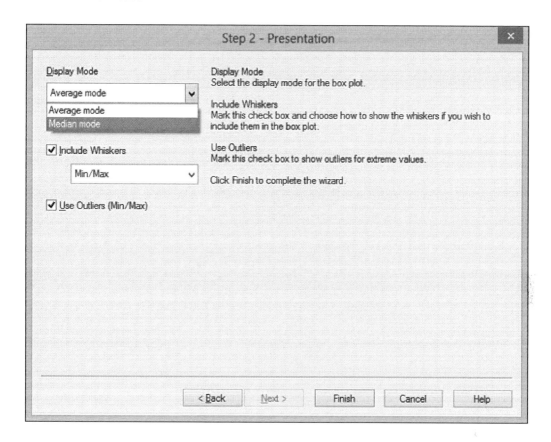

5. Select the following values:

Display Mode	Median
Include Whiskers	On or Min/Max
Use Outliers	On

6. Click on **Finish**.

How it works...

The wizard takes care of creating the expressions that will be needed for this box plot. In this case, where there is an "aggregator"; that dimension is used as part of an `Aggr` expression.

There are two approaches to the box plot that can be achieved from the wizard:

- ▶ Median mode
    - ❑ The central line is defined by the median (fiftieth percentile)
    - ❑ Top of the box is the seventy-fifth percentile
    - ❑ Bottom is the seventy-fifth percentile
    - ❑ Upper whisker is the maximum value
    - ❑ Lower whisker is the minimum value
- ▶ Average mode
    - ❑ The central line is defined by the mean value
    - ❑ Top of the box is the Mean + the Standard Deviation
    - ❑ Bottom of the box is the Mean – the Standard Deviation

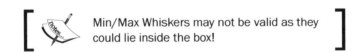 Min/Max Whiskers may not be valid as they could lie inside the box!

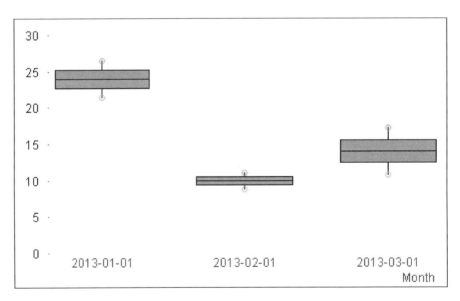

There's more...

This recipe uses the AGGR function to see the average/median values of an aggregation. However, the box plot can be used for more than averages.

See also

▸ The *Creating a box plot chart for a simple data set* recipe

Creating a "Stephen Few" bullet chart

Stephen Few designed the bullet chart as a replacement for a traditional gauge.

A traditional gauge takes up a large amount of space to encode, usually, only one value. A bullet chart is linear and can encode more than one value.

The main components of a bullet chart (from Stephen Few's `perceptualedge.com`) are as follows:

▸ A text label

▸ A quantitative scale along a single linear axis

▸ The featured measure

▸ One or two comparative measures (optional)

▸ From two to five ranges along the quantitative scale to declare the featured measure's qualitative state (optional)

There is no native bullet chart in QlikView. However, we can create one by combining a couple of objects.

Items 1, 2, 4, and 5 can be achieved with a linear gauge chart. The bar, item 3, can then be overlaid using a separate and transparent bar chart.

Getting ready

Load the following script:

```
LOAD * INLINE [
    Country, Sales, Target
    USA, 1000, 1100
    UK, 800, 1000
    Germany, 800, 700
    Japan, 1000, 1000
];
```

How to do it...

Perform the following steps to create a Stephen Few bullet chart:

1. Add a new gauge chart. You should add a title and enter text for **Title in chart**. Click on **Next**.

2. There is no dimension in this chart. Click on **Next**.

3. Enter the following expression:

   Sum(Target)

4. Click on **Next**.

5. There is no sorting (because there is no dimension), so click on **Next**.

6. On the **Style** tab, select a linear gauge and set the orientation to horizontal. Click on **Next**.

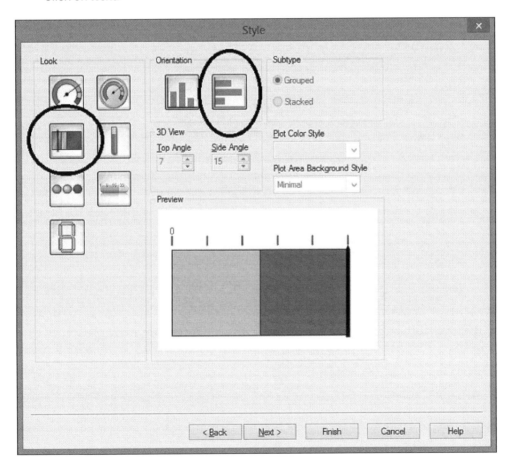

7. There are a few changes needed in the **Presentation** tab:

Gauge Settings, Max	Sum(Target) * 1.2
Indicator, Mode	Show Needle
Indicator, Style	Line
Show Scale,	
	1
Show Labels on Every	
Autowidth Segments	**Off**
Hide Segment Boundaries	**On**
Hide Gauge Outlines	**On**

8. There should be two segments by default, add a third segment by clicking on the **Add** button. The settings for each segment are as follows:

Segment 1, Lower Bound	0.0
Segment 2, Lower Bound	Sum(Target) * 0.5
Segment 3, Lower Bound	Sum(Target) * 0.9

9. Apply appropriate colors for each segment (for example, **RAG** or **Dark/Medium/ Light gray**).

10. Click on **Finish**.

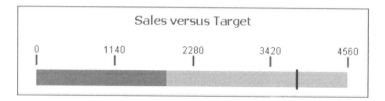

11. Most of the bullet chart elements are now in place. In fact, this type of linear chart may be enough for some uses. Now we need to add the bar chart.

12. Add a new bar chart. Don't worry about the title (it will be hidden). Turn off **Show Title in Chart**. Click on **Next**.

13. There is no dimension in this chart either. Click on **Next**.

14. Add the following expression:

Sum(Sales)

15. Click on **Next**.

16. There is no sort (as there is no dimension). Click on **Next**.

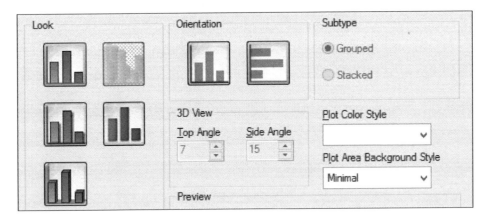

17. Select a plain bar type. The orientation should be horizontal. Leave the style at the default of **Minimal**. Click on **Next**.

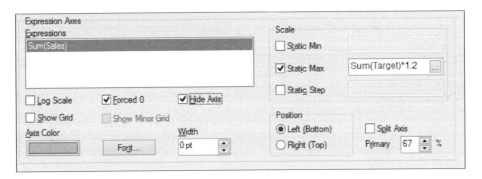

18. Set the following axis settings:

Hide Axis	**On**
Static Max	**On**
Static Max Expression	Sum(Target)*1.2

19. Click on **Next**.

20. On the **Color** tab, set **Transparency** to **100%**. Set the first color to a dark color. Click on **Next**.

21. Continue to click on **Next** until you get to the **Layout** tab. Set the shadow to **No Shadow** and the border width to 0. Set the **Layer** to **Top**. Click on **Next**.

22. Turn off the **Show Caption** option. Click on **Finish**.

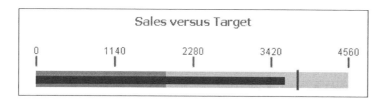

23. Position the bar chart over the gauge so that the scales match (*Ctrl* + arrow keys are useful here). The bullet chart is created.

How it works...

By matching the **Static Max** setting of the bar and the gauge (to the sum of target * 1.2), we ensure that the two charts will always size the same. The 1.2 factor makes the area beyond the target point of 20 percent of the length of the area before it. This might need to be adjusted for different implementations.

It is also crucial to ensure that the layer setting of the bar chart is at least one above the layer of the gauge chart. The default layer (on the **Layout** tab) for charts is **Normal** so, in that situation, you should change the bar chart's layer to **Top**. Otherwise, use the **Custom** option to set the layers.

There's more...

Using techniques such as this to combine multiple QlikView objects can help us create many other visualizations.

See also

▸ The *Brushing parallel coordinates* recipe
▸ The *Creating a modified bullet chart in a straight table* recipe

Creating a modified bullet chart in a straight table

The main components of a bullet chart (from Stephen Few's `perceptualedge.com`) are as follows:

- ▶ A text label
- ▶ A quantitative scale along a single linear axis
- ▶ The featured measure
- ▶ One or two comparative measures (optional)
- ▶ From two to five ranges along the quantitative scale to declare the featured measure's qualitative state (optional)

The "traditional" approach is to have bar representing the feature measure and a line representing the comparative measure. However, as long as we have two separate representations, the bar is not absolutely necessary.

In this recipe we will present a modified bullet chart using an inline linear gauge in a straight table. This allows users to view the results across all the values in a dimension.

Getting ready

Load the following script:

```
LOAD * INLINE [
    Country, Sales, Target
    USA, 1000, 1100
    UK, 800, 1000
    Germany, 800, 700
    Japan, 1000, 1000
];
```

How to do it...

Follow these steps to create a straight table with a modified bullet chart:

1. Create a new straight table. Set the dimension to be `Country`. Add three expressions:

   ```
   Sum(Sales)
   Sum(Target)
   Sum(Sales)/Sum(Target)
   ```

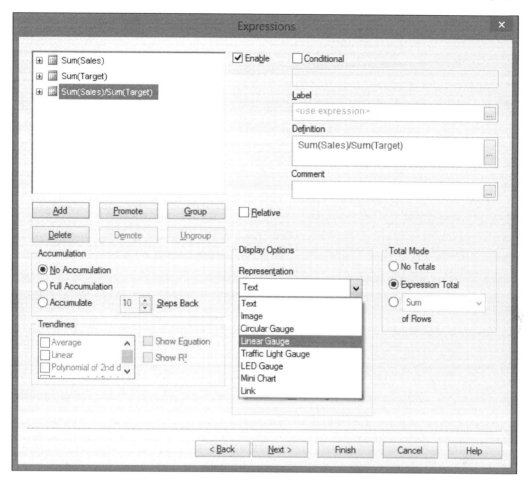

2. Change the representation of the third expression to **Linear Gauge**.

3. Click on the **Gauge Settings** button and enter the following settings for the gauge:

Guage Settings, Max	**1.5**
Indicator, Mode	**Show Needle**
Indicator, Style	**Arrow**
Show Scale	**Off**
Autowidth Segments	**Off**
Hide Segment Boundaries	**Off**
Hide Gauge Outlines	**On**

4. There should be two segments already there. Configure these settings:

Segment 1, Lower Bound	0.0
Segment 2, Lower Bound	1.0

5. Set the color of both segments to be the same. I usually go for a light gray.

6. Click on **OK**. Click on **Finish** to close the chart wizard.

Sum(Sales)			📧 XL _ ☐
Country	Sum(Sales)	Sum(Target)	Sum(Sales)/S...
	3600	3800	
Germany	800	700	
Japan	1000	1000	
UK	800	1000	
USA	1000	1100	

7. The modified bullet chart should appear in the straight table.

How it works...

Because we are calculating a percentage here, it is valid to use the same gauge for each dimension (which would not have been valid in a straight table for absolute values).

By using two segments in the linear gauge, the border between them, which we have set to 1 = 100%, presents as a line. This is our target value. The needle of the gauge displays the percentage of sales versus that target.

The user can quickly scan down the table to see the better performing territories. This field is also sortable.

There's more...

Using linear gauges in straight tables can be a great way of visually representing data. It is worth playing around with.

See also

- ▸ The *Creating a Stephen Few bullet chart* recipe
- ▸ The *Creating a bar chart in a straight table* recipe
- ▸ The *Creating a Redmond Aged Debt Profile chart* recipe

Creating a bar chart in a straight table

Straight tables are great for displaying numbers. Bar charts are great for showing the information visually. A great thing that you can do in QlikView is combine both—using linear gauges.

Getting ready

Load the following script:

```
LOAD * INLINE [
    Country, Total Debt, 0-60, 60-180, 180+
    USA, 152, 123, 23, 6
    Canada, 250, 100, 100, 50
    UK, 170, 170, 0, 0
    Germany, 190, 0, 0, 190
    Japan, 90, 15, 25, 50
    France, 225, 77, 75, 73
];
```

How to do it...

Use these steps to create a straight table containing a bar chart:

1. Create a new straight table. Set the dimension to be Country. Add two expressions:

   ```
   Sum([Total Debt])
   Sum([Total Debt]) /
   Max(Total Aggr(Sum([Total Debt]), Country))
   ```

2. Set the **Total Mode** property of the second expression to **No Totals**.

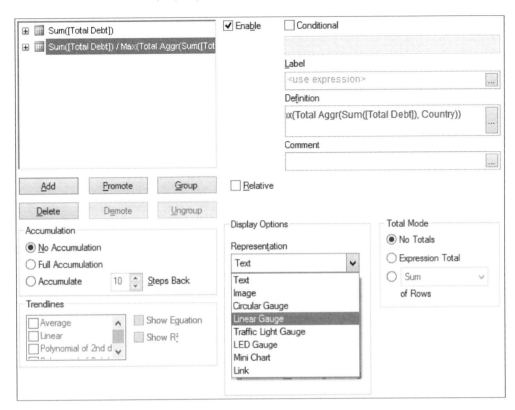

3. Change the **Representation** property of the second expression to **Linear Gauge**.

4. Click on the **Gauge Settings** button and enter the following settings for the gauge:

Guage Settings, Max	**1**
Indicator, Mode	**Fill to Value**
Indicator, Style	**Arrow**
Show Scale	**Off**
Autowidth Segments	**On**
Hide Segment Boundaries	**On**
Hide Gauge Outlines	**On**

5. There should be two segments already there. Remove Segment 2, leaving only 1.

6. Set the color of the segment to an appropriate color. Pastels work well here.

7. Click on **OK**. Click on **Finish** to close the chart wizard.

Country	Sum([Total...	Sum([Total Debt])...
	1077	
Canada	250	
France	225	
Germany	190	
UK	170	
USA	152	
Japan	90	

How it works...

The AGGR expression returns the maximum value across all the countries. In this example, 250 from Canada. If we then divide the total debt for each country by this maximum value, we will get a ratio with a maximum value of 1. This is exactly what we need to create the bar chart with the linear gauge.

There's more...

This technique can be utilized anywhere that you need to create a bar chart in a table such as this. The added visual can really bring the numbers to light.

See also

- ▶ The *Creating a modified bullet chart in a straight table* recipe
- ▶ The *Creating a Redmond Aged Debt Profile chart* recipe

Creating a Redmond Aged Debt Profile chart

I can't claim that I really created this general type of chart. Someone once said, there is nothing new under the sun. I know that other people have created similar stuff. However, I did create this implementation in QlikView to solve a real business problem for a customer and couldn't find anything exactly like it anywhere else.

This recipe follows on from the previous one (it uses the same data). We are going to extend the straight table to add additional bars to represent the aged debt profile.

Getting ready

Create the straight table from the previous recipe.

How to do it...

Follow these steps to create a Redmond Aged Debt Profile chart:

1. Open the properties of the chart and go to the **Expressions** tab. Right-click on the second expression and select **Copy** from the menu:

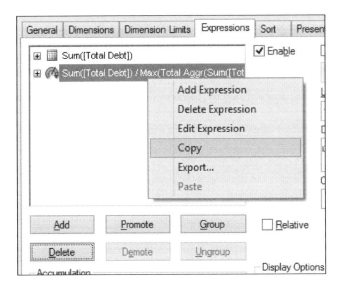

2. Right-click in the blank area below the expressions and select **Paste**. This will create a new expression with the same properties as the copy:

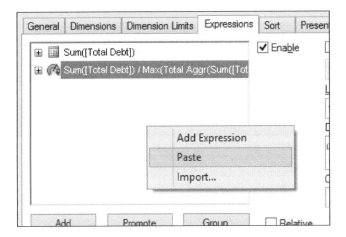

3. Repeat the paste operation two more times to create three copies in total.

4. Modify the three expressions as follows:

```
Sum([0-60])/Sum([Total Debt])
Sum([60-180])/Sum([Total Debt])
Sum([180+])/Sum([Total Debt])
```

5. Click on the **Gauge Settings** buttons for each and choose a different color from the original bar.

6. Click on **OK** when done.

Total Debt				
Country	Total Debt	0-60	60-180	180+
	1077			
Canada	250			
France	225			
Germany	190			
UK	170			
USA	152			
Japan	90			

How it works...

The first column is a bar chart representing the vertical distribution of the total debt for each country. In the three following period columns, we divide each period value by the total debt for that country to get the ratio—the horizontal distribution of that country's debt across the periods. This allows the user to quickly scan down the chart and see which countries have the highest percentage debt in each period.

There's more...

There a many more situations where this can be used. Anywhere that you might consider using a stacked bar chart, consider using a Redmond instead.

See also

▶ The *Creating a modified bullet chart in a straight table* recipe

Creating a waterfall chart

A waterfall chart is a type of bar chart used to show a whole value and the breakdown of that value into other subvalues, all in one chart. We can implement it in QlikView using the **Bar Offset** option.

In this example, we are going to demonstrate the chart showing a profit and loss breakdown.

Getting ready

Load the following script:

```
LOAD * INLINE [
    Category, Value
    Sales, 62000
    COGS, 25000
    Expenses, 27000
    Tax, 3000
];
```

How to do it...

The following steps show you how to create a waterfall chart:

1. Create a new bar chart. There is no dimension in this chart. We need to add three expressions:

Sales $	Sum({<Category={'Sales'}>} Value)
COGS $	Sum({<Category={'COGS'}>} Value)
Expenses $	Sum({<Category={'Expenses'}>} Value)
Tax $	Sum({<Category={'Tax'}>} Value)
	Sum({<Category={'Sales'}>} Value)
Net Profit $	-Sum({<Category={'COGS','Expenses', 'Tax'}>} Value)

2. Once you have added the expressions, click on **Finish**.

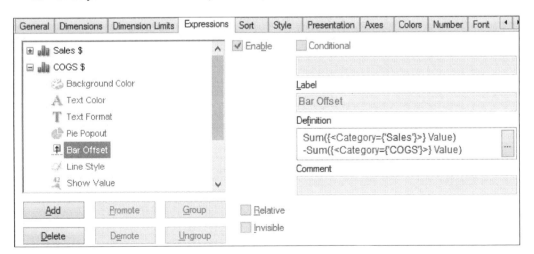

3. Edit the properties of the chart. On the **Expressions** tab, click on the + sign beside the **COGS $** expression. Click on the **Bar Offset** option. Enter the following expression into the **Definition** box:

```
Sum({<Category={'Sales'}>} Value)
-Sum({<Category={'COGS'}>} Value)
```

4. Repeat for the **Expenses $** expression. Enter the following expression for the **Bar Offset**:

```
Sum({<Category={'Sales'}>} Value)
-Sum({<Category={'COGS', 'Expenses'}>} Value)
```

5. Repeat once more for the **Tax $** expression. Enter the following expression for the bar offset:

```
Sum({<Category={'Sales'}>} Value)
-Sum({<Category={'COGS', 'Expenses', 'Tax'}>} Value)
```

6. Click on **OK** to save the changes.

7. The waterfall chart should look like the following screenshot:

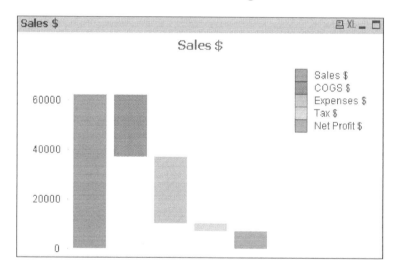

How it works...

The **Bar Offset** option for bar charts allows us to calculate the start position for each of the bars, other than the 0 default value.

We use a Set Analysis expression to easily calculate the values.

While this example is reasonably trivial, it is reflective of a real-life example and there are many others. Using `Set Analysis` functions to calculate the value for the offset is very typical.

Replacing the legend in a line chart with labels on each line

One of the problems with a standard QlikView line chart is that the legend is somewhat removed from the chart, and it can be difficult to keep going back and forth between the legend and the data to work out which line is which.

A way of resolving this is to remove the legend and replace it with labels on each line.

Getting ready

Load the following script:

```
CrossTable(Country, Sales)
LOAD * INLINE [
    Date, USA, UK, Japan, Germany
    2013-01-01, 123, 100, 80, 40
    2013-02-01, 134, 111, 75, 50
    2013-03-01, 155,  95, 70, 60
    2013-04-01, 165,  85, 88, 50
    2013-05-01, 154, 125, 90, 70
    2013-06-01, 133, 110, 75, 99
];
```

How to do it...

These steps will create a line chart with labels on each line instead of a legend:

1. Add a new line chart. Add two dimensions, `Date` and `Country`.

2. Add the following expression:

```
Dual(
    If(Date=Max(total Date), Country, ''),
    Sum(Sales)
)
```

3. On the **Expressions** tab, ensure that the **Values on Data Points** option is checked.

4. Click on **Next** until you get to the **Presentation** tab. Deselect the **Show Legend** option.

5. Click on **Finish** on the wizard.

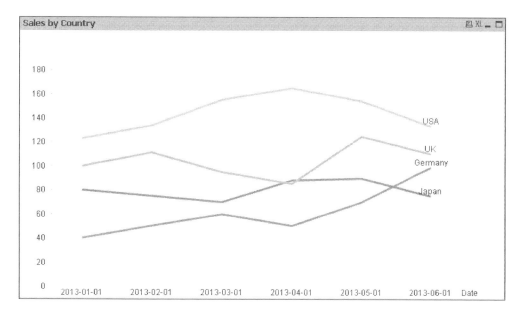

How it works...

The `Dual` function will only return a text value when the date matches the maximum date. Otherwise, it is blank. So, when we enable the **Values on Data Points** option, it only displays a value for the last data point.

It is critical that you don't set a number format for the expression. The **Expression Default** option means that it will use the text from the dual.

There's more...

Dual is a really useful function to allow us to define exactly what will be displayed on labels such as this. It is also really useful for sorting text values in a specific order.

See also

▶ The *Staggering labels in a pie chart* recipe

Creating a secondary dimension in a bar chart

Within QlikView, there is the possibility of displaying a secondary *X*-axis in a bar chart. This can be useful for displaying some hierarchical data, for example, year and month. In fact, it only really works where there is a strict hierarchy such as this. Each of the secondary values would exist in each of the primary values (as each month occurs in each year).

Getting ready

Load the following script:

```
CrossTable(Year, Sales)
LOAD * INLINE [
    Month, 2011, 2012, 2013
    1, 123, 233, 376
    2, 423, 355, 333
    3, 212, 333, 234
    4, 344, 423
    5, 333, 407
    6, 544, 509
    7, 634, 587
    8, 322, 225
    9, 452, 523
    10, 478, 406
    11, 679, 765
    12, 521, 499
];
```

How to do it...

Follow these steps to create a bar chart with a secondary dimension:

1. Create a new bar chart with `Year` and `Month` as dimensions and the expression:

   `Sum(Sales)`

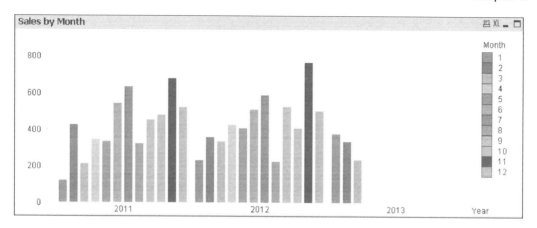

 Note that this chart shows the monthly trend.

2. Edit the chart and add a second expression with just a value of **0**:

3. A new legend will appear.

4. Open the properties and go to the **Presentation** tab. Deselect the **Show Legend** option:

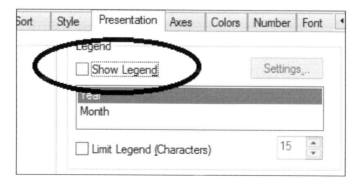

Note that all subvalues (months) are displayed under all the primary values (years).

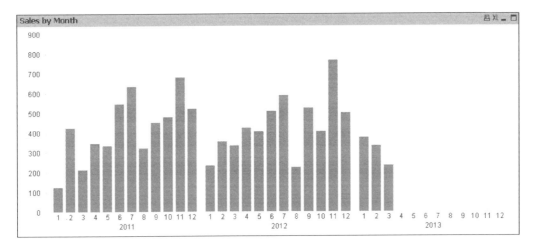

5. Edit the properties of the chart and go to the **Axes** tab. Set the **Secondary Dimension Labels** to the / option as shown in the following screenshot:

Note that the labels for the secondary dimension are now at an angle:

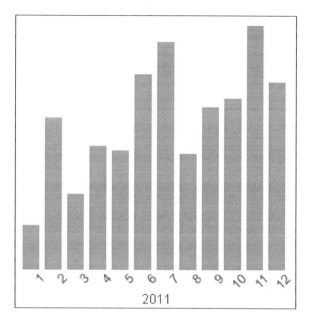

How it works...

QlikView will automatically add the secondary dimension to a bar chart when:

- ▸ There are more than two dimensions
- ▸ There are two dimensions and there are two or more bar expressions

If there are two expressions, the bars will automatically stack. By setting an expression with a value of 0, the second bars will not appear. However, we do need to remove the legend.

There's more...

This can be useful in a number of situations. However, as previously noted, the two dimensions must be in a strict hierarchy. If there are values that don't exist under all the primary dimensions, they will be represented under all of them anyway and that may not achieve the results that you were hoping for.

Creating a line chart with variable width lines

This is an interesting technique that has some rare enough applications. However, it could be a useful one to have in your arsenal.

I used it to create my *Homage to Minard* (`http://qliktips.blogspot.ie/2012/06/homage-to-minard.html`).

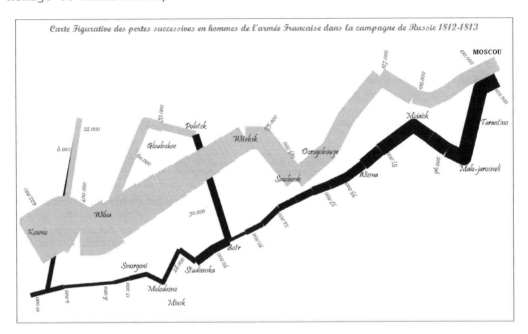

Getting ready

Load the following script:

```
LOAD * INLINE [
    Country, Sales, Target, Month
    USA, 1000, 1500, 2013-01-01
    USA, 1200, 1600, 2013-02-01
    USA, 3500, 1800, 2013-03-01
    USA, 2500, 2000, 2013-04-01
    USA, 3000, 2500, 2013-05-01
    USA, 2500, 3000, 2013-06-01
    UK, 1000, 1500, 2013-01-01
    UK, 1700, 1600, 2013-02-01
```

```
    UK, 2200, 1800, 2013-03-01
    UK, 2000, 2000, 2013-04-01
    UK, 1300, 2500, 2013-05-01
    UK, 1900, 3000, 2013-06-01
];
```

How to do it...

These steps will show you how to create a line chart with variable width lines:

1. Create a new line chart. Add `Month` and `Country` as dimensions.

2. On the **Expressions** tab, add this expression:

   ```
   Sum(Sales)
   ```

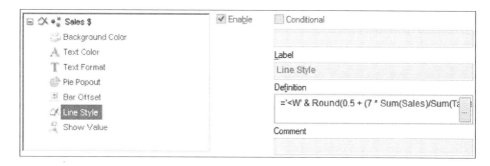

3. Click on the + sign beside the expression and enter this expression for the **Line Style** property:

   ```
   ='<W' &
   Round(0.5 + (7 * Sum(Sales)/Sum(Target)), 0.1)
   & '>'
   ```

4. Still on the **Expressions** tab, in the **Display Options** section, select **Symbol** and select **Dots** from the drop-down menu:

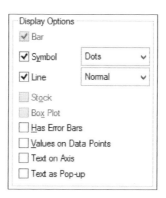

5. Set the **Line Width** property to **1 pt** and the **Symbol Size** property to **2 pt**. Click on **Finish**:

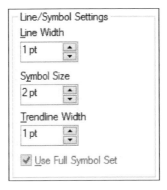

6. The chart shows the values as normal; however, the lines are thicker where performance versus target is better:

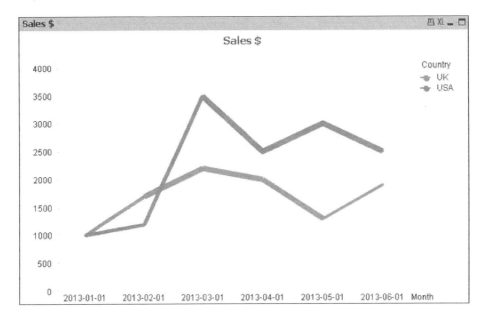

How it works...

The **Line Style** property allows you to specify a width attribute for the line chart. This is a tag in the format:

```
<Wn.n>
```

Where, `n.n` is a number between 0.5 and 8.0.

We use the `Round` function here to round the value down to one decimal place.

We add the dots style symbol because they help fill in some gaps in the lines, especially where there are sharper corners.

There's more...

There are a few applications of this. In the same blog post as the Minard chart, I have shown an image of a chart using this function and a smooth line option.

Brushing parallel coordinates

Parallel coordinates is a long established method of visualizing multivariate data. QlikView will display a parallel coordinate chart and a user can interact with the data, but sometimes it is useful to allow the user to "brush" the data, selecting different values and seeing those values versus the whole of the data.

We can do this by using two almost identical charts with one being transparent and sitting over the other.

Getting ready

We need to download some data for this from the United States Census QuickFacts website. Go to `http://quickfacts.census.gov/qfd/download_data.html` and download the first three files on offer:

Files	Description
DataSet.txt	Raw data
DataDict.txt	Information on the different metrics in the raw data
FIPS_CountyName.txt	List of the U.S. counties

Load the following script:

```
// Cross table the raw data into a temp table
Temp_Data:
CrossTable(MetricCode, Value)
LOAD *
FROM
```

```
DataSet.txt
(txt, codepage is 1252, embedded labels, delimiter is ',', msq);


// Load the temp table into our data table.
// Only load county information.
// Only load RHI data (Resident Population).
Data:
NoConcatenate
Load
  fips,
  MetricCode,
  Value
Resident Temp_Data
Where Mod(fips, 1000) <> 0  // Only County
And MetricCode Like 'RHI*'; // Only RHI


// Drop the temporary table
Drop Table Temp_Data;


// Load the location information.
// Use LEFT to only load locations that match Data.
Location:
Left Keep (Data)
LOAD @1:5 as fips,
     @6:n as Location
FROM
FIPS_CountyName.txt
(fix, codepage is 1252);


// Load the Metric information
// Use LEFT to only load metrics that match Data.
Metrics:
Left Keep (Data)
LOAD @1:10 As MetricCode,
     Trim(SubField(SubField(@11:115, ':', 2), ',', 1)) as Metric,
     @116:119 as Unit,
     @120:128 as Decimal,
     @129:140 as US_Total,
     @141:152 as Minimum,
     @153:164 as Maximum,
     @165:n as Source
FROM
DataDict.txt
(fix, codepage is 1252, embedded labels);
```

How to do it...

To create a parallel coordinates chart with brushing, perform the following steps:

1. Add a list box for **Location** onto the layout.

2. Create a new line chart. Add `Metric` and `Location` as dimensions.

3. Add the following expression:

   ```
   Avg({<Location={*}>} Value)
   ```

4. Label the expression as `%`.

5. Click on the + sign beside the expression and enter the following expression for **Background Color**:

   ```
   LightGray()
   ```

6. On the **Sort** tab, set the sort for the **Metric** dimension to **Load Order** and **Original** as shown in the following screenshot:

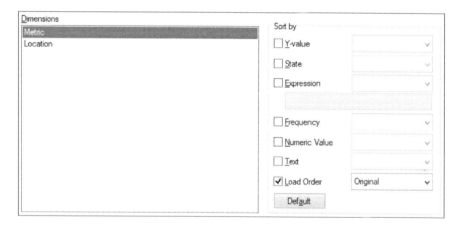

7. On the **Presentation** tab, turn off the **Suppress Zero-Values** and **Suppress Missing** options. Also, turn off the **Show Legend** option:

8. On the **Axes** tab, turn on the **Static Max** option and set it to 101. Set the **Primary Dimension Labels** option to /. Turn on the **Show Grid** option under **Dimension Axis**:

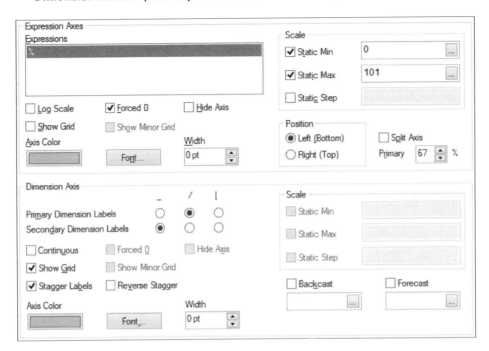

9. Click on **Finish**.

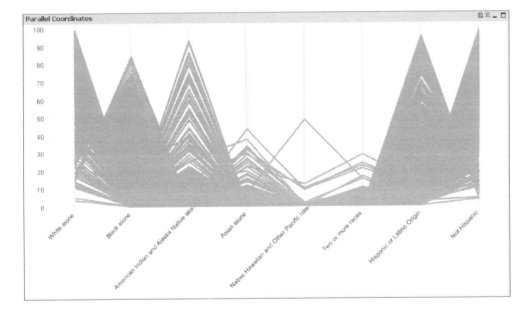

10. Right-click on the chart and select **Clone** from the menu. Position the new chart so it exactly overlaps the first. Edit the properties.

11. On the **Expressions** tab, modify the expression:

```
Avg(Value)
```

12. Click on the + sign beside the expression and change the **Background Color** property to:

```
Blue()
```

13. On the **Colors** tab, set the **Transparency** option to `100%`.

14. On the **Layout** tab, set the **Layer** option to **Top**. Set the **Show** option to **Conditional** and enter the following expression:

```
GetSelectedCount(Location)>0
```

15. Click on **OK**.

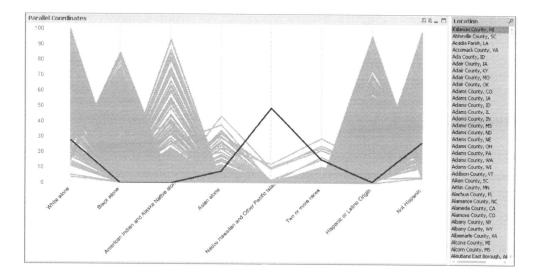

Note that when you make a selection on the chart or in the list box, the selection is highlighted or "brushed".

How it works...

The transparent chart with the slightly different color and expression is the trick here. When a selection is made, our chart overlays the first chart and displays the "brush". The underlying chart will remain the same as we have a set that excludes selections in the **Location** field.

As far as the user is concerned, there is only one chart being displayed.

There's more...

Using transparent charts to overlay another chart is a great technique to use when the particular visualization is just not available in QlikView.

See also

▸ The *Creating a "Stephen Few" bullet chart* recipe

Using redundant encoding with a scatter chart

It is very typical to display values for categorical dimensions using a bar chart. This is a very powerful and simple way to understand a chart. The length of the bars models the values in a very intuitive way.

Sometimes, however, it can be valuable to add an additional level of encoding to gain additional insight.

In this example, we are going to add space as an additional encoding. We can do this using a scatter chart.

Getting ready

Load the following script:

```
LOAD * INLINE [
    Country, Sales
    USA, 100000
    UK, 60000
```

```
    Germany, 50000
    France, 45000
    Canada, 30000
    Mexico, 20000
    Japan, 15000
];
```

How to do it...

Use the following steps to create a scatter chart demonstrating redundant encoding:

1. Create a new scatter chart.

2. Add a calculated dimension with the following expression:

   ```
   =ValueList(1,2)
   ```

3. Deselect the **Label** and **Show Legend** options for this dimension.

4. Add Country as the second dimension.

5. On the **Expressions** tab, add two expressions:

   ```
   Sum(Sales)
   If(ValueList(1,2)=1, 0, Sum(Sales))
   ```

6. Both expressions can be labeled as **Sales $**:

7. On the **Sort** tab, select the **Country** dimension and turn on the **Expression** option. Enter the expression:

   ```
   Sum(Sales)
   ```

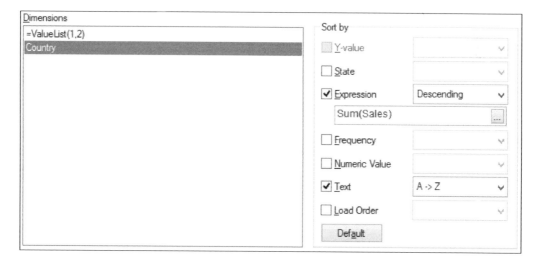

8. The direction should be **Descending**.

9. Go onto the **Axes** tab and select **Hide Axis** under the **X Axis** options.

10. On the **Numbers** tab, format both expressions as **Integer**.

11. Click on **Finish**.

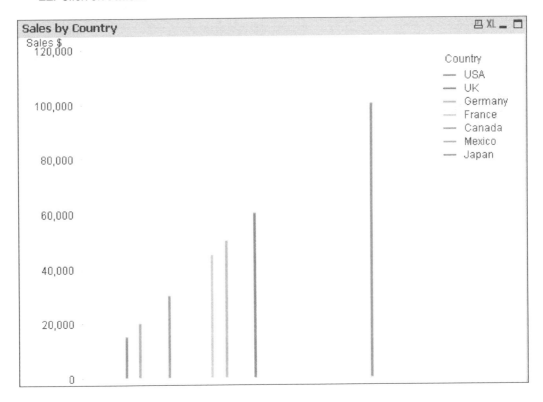

12. The chart displays with apparent bars and spacing between them. We can quickly see how much bigger the gap is between the USA and other countries. We can also identify clusters of similarly performing countries.

How it works...

If a scatter chart has two dimensions, it will change from displaying bubbles to displaying lines between the values in the first dimension.

The first expression here positions where the bars will exist. It is our space encoding.

The second expression has a test to see if it is ValueList = 1, which sets a value of 0, or ValueList = 2, which sets the `Sales $` value.

There's more...

This is an example of the use of pseudo dimensions using `ValueList`. This can be a very powerful function in dimensions.

The more frequent first dimension of a multidimensional scatter chart would be a date dimension, such as a year. This gives you the option to show lines going from year to year. Additional options in **Presentation** allow such items as arrows.

Staggering labels in a pie chart

I am not a big fan of using pie charts for many segments. The more segments that there are, the less easy it is to see the data. As the segments get smaller, even the labels get smudged into each other.

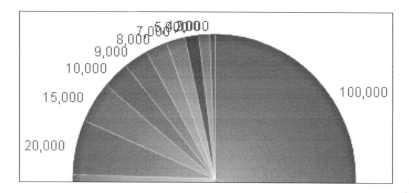

If you absolutely, positively must create this type of chart, you need to have a better strategy for the labels.

Getting ready

Load the following script:

```
LOAD * INLINE [
      Country, Sales
      USA, 100000
      Canada, 50000
      Mexico, 25000
      UK, 70000
      Germany, 20000
      Brazil, 15000
      France, 10000
      Japan, 9000
      China, 8000
      Australia, 7000
      South Korea, 5000
      New Zealand, 4000
      Italy, 2000
];
```

How to do it...

Follow these steps to create a pie chart with staggered labels:

1. Create a new pie chart.

2. Add Country as the dimension.

3. On the **Expressions** tab, add the following expression:

    ```
    Dual(
       Country & '-' &
       Num(sum(Sales), '#,##0') &
       Repeat(chr(13)&chr(10), rank(Sum(Sales))-6),
       sum(Sales)
    )
    ```

4. Select the **Values on Data Points** option.

5. On the **Sort** tab, select the **Y-Value** option. Confirm **Descending** as the direction.

6. On the **Presentation** tab, deselect the **Show Legend** option.

7. Click on **Finish**.

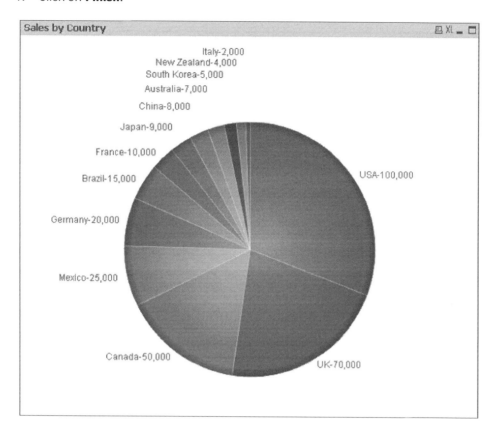

8. Resize the chart so that all the values can be seen.

How it works...

The magic here is the Repeat function:

```
Repeat(chr(13)&chr(10), rank(Sum(Sales))-6)
```

The ASCII characters 13 and 10 give us a carriage return and line feed. Note that there is a Rank()-6 here. Basically, the repeat doesn't kick in until you get to the seventh ranked value in the dimension. There is no reason to start staggering for the earlier values.

There's more...

This is the only time that I have actually had to use the `Repeat` function in a chart. It does have uses in the frontend in `Text` objects. Mostly, it would be used in the script to generate data.

Creating dynamic ad hoc analysis in QlikView

QlikView has some great tools to allow users to generate their own content. However, sometimes users don't want to learn those skills and would like to quickly just to be able to analyze data.

In this recipe, we will show how to create an easy-to-use dynamic analysis tool using some of the features from QlikView 11.

Getting ready

Load the following script:

```
// Set the Hide Prefix
Set HidePrefix='%';

// Load the list of dimensions
DimensionList:
Load * Inline [
  %Dimensions
  SalesPerson
  Country
  City
  Product
];

// Load the list of expressions
ExpressionList:
Load * Inline [
  %ExpressionName
  Total Sales
  Order Count
  Avg. Sales
];
```

```
// Load the Sales data
Data:
LOAD * INLINE [
    SalesPerson, Country, City, Product, Sales, Orders
    Joe, Germany, Berlin, Bricks, 129765, 399
    Joe, Germany, Berlin, Brogues, 303196, 5842
    Joe, Germany, Berlin, Widgets, 64358, 1603
    Joe, Germany, Berlin, Woggles, 120587, 670
    Joe, Germany, Frankfurt, Bricks, 264009, 2327
    Joe, Germany, Frankfurt, Brogues, 369565, 3191
    Joe, Germany, Frankfurt, Widgets, 387441, 5331
    Joe, Germany, Frankfurt, Woggles, 392757, 735
    Joe, Germany, Munich, Bricks, 153952, 1937
    Joe, Germany, Munich, Brogues, 319644, 645
    Joe, Germany, Munich, Widgets, 47616, 2820
    Joe, Germany, Munich, Woggles, 105483, 3205
    Brian, Japan, Osaka, Bricks, 17086, 281
    Brian, Japan, Osaka, Brogues, 339902, 2872
    Brian, Japan, Osaka, Widgets, 148935, 1864
    Brian, Japan, Osaka, Woggles, 142033, 2085
    Brian, Japan, Tokyo, Bricks, 161972, 1707
    Brian, Japan, Tokyo, Brogues, 387405, 2992
    Brian, Japan, Tokyo, Widgets, 270573, 3212
    Brian, Japan, Tokyo, Woggles, 134713, 5522
    Brian, Japan, Yokohama, Bricks, 147943, 4595
    Brian, Japan, Yokohama, Brogues, 405429, 6844
    Brian, Japan, Yokohama, Widgets, 266462, 3158
    Brian, Japan, Yokohama, Woggles, 477315, 5802
    Joe, UK, Birmingham, Bricks, 23150, 1754
    Joe, UK, Birmingham, Brogues, 200568, 1763
    Joe, UK, Birmingham, Widgets, 262824, 617
    Joe, UK, Birmingham, Woggles, 173118, 5359
    Joe, UK, London, Bricks, 621409, 712
    Joe, UK, London, Brogues, 504268, 2873
    Joe, UK, London, Widgets, 260335, 1313
    Joe, UK, London, Woggles, 344435, 743
    Joe, UK, Manchester, Bricks, 401928, 1661
    Joe, UK, Manchester, Brogues, 7366, 2530
    Joe, UK, Manchester, Widgets, 6108, 5106
    Joe, UK, Manchester, Woggles, 269611, 4344
    Mary, USA, Boston, Bricks, 442658, 3374
    Mary, USA, Boston, Brogues, 147127, 3129
    Mary, USA, Boston, Widgets, 213802, 1604
    Mary, USA, Boston, Woggles, 395072, 1157
```

```
        Michael, USA, Dallas, Bricks, 499805, 3378
        Michael, USA, Dallas, Brogues, 354623, 18
        Michael, USA, Dallas, Widgets, 422612, 2130
        Michael, USA, Dallas, Woggles, 217603, 2612
        Mary, USA, New York, Bricks, 313600, 6468
        Mary, USA, New York, Brogues, 559745, 1743
        Mary, USA, New York, Widgets, 94558, 2910
        Mary, USA, New York, Woggles, 482012, 3173
        Michael, USA, San Diego, Bricks, 95594, 4214
        Michael, USA, San Diego, Brogues, 24639, 3337
        Michael, USA, San Diego, Widgets, 107683, 5257
        Michael, USA, San Diego, Woggles, 221065, 5058
    ];
```

How to do it...

These steps show you how to create dynamic ad hoc analysis in QlikView:

1. Open the **Select Fields** tab of the sheet properties. Select on the **Show System Fields** option (so you can see the hidden fields). Add a list box on the display for the **%Dimensions** and **%ExpressionName** fields.

2. Create a new bar chart.

3. Set the title of the chart to `Sales Analysis`. Turn on **Fast Type Change** for **Bar Chart**, **Pie Chart**, **Straight Table**, and **Block Chart**. Click on **Next**.

4. Add the four dimensions – `Country`, `City`, `Product`, and `SalesPerson`. For each dimension, turn on **Enable Condition** and set the following expressions for each of them:

Dimension	Expression

Country	`=Alt(`
	`    WildMatch(`
	`        GetFieldSelections(%Dimensions, '|'),`
	`        '*Country*')`
	`    ,0)`

City	`=Alt(`
	`    WildMatch(`
	`        GetFieldSelections(%Dimensions, '|'),`
	`        '*City*')`
	`    ,0`

Dimension	Expression
Product	```=Alt(` ` WildMatch(` ` GetFieldSelections(%Dimensions, '|'),` ` '*Product*')` ` ,0)```
SalesPerson	```=Alt(` ` WildMatch(` ` GetFieldSelections(%Dimensions, '|'),` ` '*SalesPerson*')` ` ,0)```

5. Add the following three expressions and set Conditional on each of them:

Expression	Conditional Expression
Sum(Sales)	```=Alt(` ` WildMatch(` ` GetFieldSelections(` ` %ExpressionName, '|'),` ` '*Total Sales*')` ` , 0)```
Sum(Orders)	```=Alt(` ` WildMatch(` ` GetFieldSelections(` ` %ExpressionName, '|'),` ` '*Order Count*')` ` , 0)```
Sum(Sales)/ Sum(Orders)	```=Alt(` ` WildMatch(` ` GetFieldSelections(` ` %ExpressionName, '|'),` ` '*Avg. Sales*')` ` , 0)```

6. On the **Style** tab, set the orientation to **Horizontal**.

7. On the **Presentation** tab, turn on the **Enable X-Axis Scrollbar** option and set **When Number of Items Exceeds** to 8.

8. On the **Layout** tab, deselect the **Size to Data** option.

9. On the **Caption** tab, turn off the **Allow Minimize** and **Allow Maximize** options. Click on **Finish**.

10. Add a list box for the four main dimensions. Add a container object for the four list boxes. Add a **Current Selections** box.

11. Lay the objects out for ease of use.

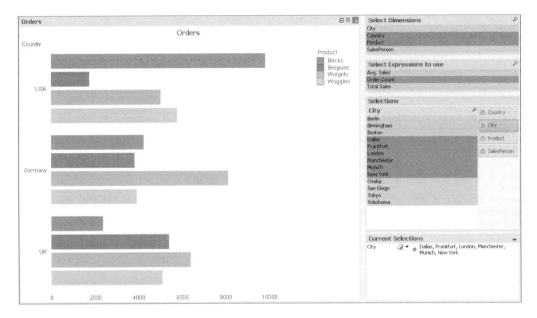

How it works...

There are a couple of things going on here.

First, in the load script, we are setting a `HidePrefix` variable. Once this is set, any field that has this value as its prefix will become a hidden or system field. The benefit of using this for our dimension and expression selectors is that any selections in hidden fields will not appear in the **Current Selections** box.

The next thing that concerns us is the conditional functions. I am using the `GetFieldSelections` function to return the list of values that are selected. We use `WildMatch` to check if our dimension or expression should be shown. The whole expression is wrapped in an `Alt` function because if there are no values selected at all, the `GetFieldSelections` function returns null, so we need to return 0 in that case.

There's more...

There is a lot of scope for this to be extended. I have only included one chart here and you could use multiple charts and have multiple different options for selections.

2
Layout

In this chapter, we will cover:

- ▸ Changing the default object layout options
- ▸ Changing the default selection color scheme
- ▸ Modifying the green, white, and gray selection color schemes
- ▸ Modifying the green, white, and gray selection color schemes on QlikView Server
- ▸ Using containers as an alternative to multi-boxes
- ▸ Using the design menus to custom format a cell

Introduction

There are some best practices that one should always follow when creating a layout in QlikView.

For general advice on visualizing data, I recommend the following people:

Name	Publication	Website
Stephen Few	Show Me The Numbers, Information Dashboard Design, and Now You See It.	www.perceptualedge.com
Robert Kosara	Eager Eyes Blog	www.eagereyes.org
Andy Kirk	Data Visualization: a successful design process	www.visualisingdata.com
Alberto Cairo	The Functional Art	www.thefunctionalart.com

There are, of course, many others on note, but the list could go for several pages and you wouldn't get to the bottom of it!

My purpose in this chapter is to show you how to layout and configure documents so that you can implement best practices.

Changing the default object layout options

The default layout option in QlikView is **Simplified**. When you look at the **Layout** tab of any object, you will only see, two options on the left-hand side: **Shadow Intensity** and **Border Width**:

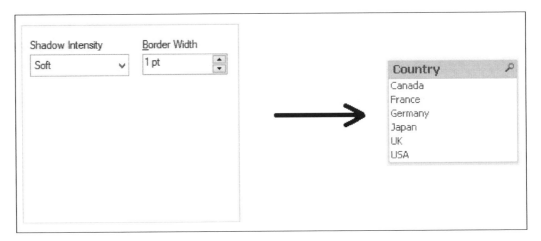

While these options suffice for 99 percent of all layouts, there are many other options that we can make available to us, if required.

Getting ready

Open any existing QlikView document with at least one listbox (perhaps one of the documents from *Chapter 1, Charts*).

How to do it...

Follow these steps to change the default layout options:

1. From the **Settings** menu, click on **Document Properties** (*Ctrl + Alt + D*).

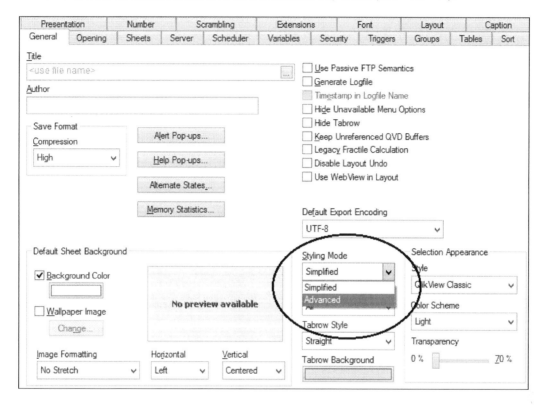

2. On the **General** tab, set the **Styling Mode** to **Advanced**. Click on **OK** to close the properties.

3. Notice that the sheet objects have changed already, probably with rounded corners.

4. Open the properties of any object and look at the **Layout** tab. Notice that there are now many more options.

5. Modify the options and notice what happens.

How it works...

Enabling the **Advanced** styling mode, opens up the option of modifying several aspects of screen objects.

In my opinion, it is unfortunate that you just can't do this for one object, because I prefer the simple look and feel that you get with the **Simple** styling mode.

You should note that with the **Simple** mode, the color of the border is simply matched automatically to the color of the caption. In **Advanced**, you have the control of the border color and that can be different to the caption color. You need to be careful with this if you have different colors for selected and non-selected objects.

See also

▸ The *Changing the default selection color scheme* recipe

Changing the default selection color scheme

QlikView has six precanned color schemes, such as **Classic**, **Forest**, **Spring**, **Lime**, **Classic Extended**, and **Light**. Out of box, the default selection color scheme is **Light**. The **Possible** options have white background, the **Selected** options are green, and the **Excluded** options have a very light gray.

On some displays, especially projectors or plasma screens, the colors do not come out as well; especially the light gray can look almost white.

Also, business users sometimes request that the color scheme be changed. While it is not straightforward to change from the green/white/gray options, there are several options to choose from (as long as they are green/white/gray!).

Getting ready

Open any existing QlikView document with at least one listbox (perhaps one of the documents from *Chapter 1, Charts*).

How to do it...

These steps will show you how to change the default color scheme:

1. From the **Settings** menu, click on **Document Properties** (*Ctrl + Alt + D*).

2. On the **General** tab, set the **Color Scheme** to **Classic**.
3. Note that the gray color in **Classic** mode is much darker. This looks much better on projectors and some plasma screens.
4. Experiment with the different options and note the changes. Also note what happens if you lock selections.

How it works...

This is a fairly straightforward option in the **Document Properties** tab that is useful to know about.

There's more...

These color scheme choices are all great, as long as you and your end users like green/white/gray (and blue) as selection colors.

Because QlikView has a brand with these colors, they are not keen on making it easy for anyone to change them, but it is possible.

See also

▶ The *Changing the default object layout options* section

▶ The *Modifying the green, white, and gray selection color schemes* recipe.

Modifying the green, white, and gray selection color schemes

QlikView selection colors are green/white/gray. They have a brand around this and are not keen for anyone who can change them.

It is, however, possible to do so. We will use the QlikView API to modify the user's color preferences.

Getting ready

Open any existing QlikView document with at least one listbox (perhaps one of the documents from *Chapter 1, Charts*).

How to do it

Follow these steps to change the default green, white, and gray color schemes:

1. From the **Tools** menu, select **Edit Module** (or press *Ctrl + M*).
2. Enter the following code:

```
Sub SetColorPrefs()

  Dim UserPrefs

  set UserPrefs = _
    ActiveDocument.GetApplication.GetUserPreferences

  ' Set the "Selected" Color
  UserPrefs.CustomSelBgColor(1).PrimaryCol.Col = _
    RGB(0,0,255)      ' Blue
  UserPrefs.CustomSelFgColor(1).PrimaryCol.Col = _
    RGB(255,255,0)    ' Yellow
  ' Set the "Possible" Color
  UserPrefs.CustomSelBgColor(2).PrimaryCol.Col = _
    RGB(255,255,0)    ' Yellow
  UserPrefs.CustomSelFgColor(2).PrimaryCol.Col = _
    RGB(0,0,0)        ' Black
```

```
' Set the Excluded Color
UserPrefs.CustomSelBgColor(5).PrimaryCol.Col = _
   RGB (200,200,200) ' Light gray
UserPrefs.CustomSelFgColor(5).PrimaryCol.Col = _
   RGB (0,0,0)  ' Black

' Set the Locked Color
UserPrefs.CustomSelBgColor(0).PrimaryCol.Col = _
   RGB (255,0,0) ' Red
UserPrefs.CustomSelFgColor(0).PrimaryCol.Col = _
   RGB (0,0,0)  ' Black

ActiveDocument.GetApplication.SetUserPreferences _
   UserPrefs

end sub
```

3.   Click on the **Check** button to test for syntax errors. It should display "***** Ready *****".

4.   Click on the **Test** button to execute the code.

5.   Click on **OK** to close the editor.

6.   From the **Settings** menu, open **Document Properties** (or press *Ctrl + Alt + D*).

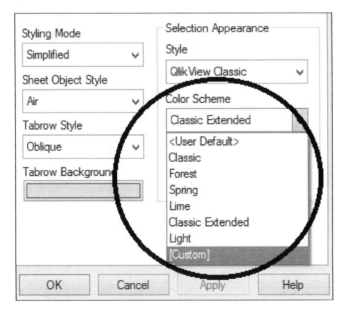

7.   Under **Color Scheme**, select **[Custom]**. Click on **OK**.

8.   Note that the new color scheme has been applied.

How it works...

The API call assigns a `UserPreferences` object to a variable, which allows us to modify each of the background and foreground colors for the following indexes:

Index	Selection State
0	Locked
1	Selected
2	Possible
3	Deselected
4	Alternative
5	Excluded
6	Excluded Selected
7	Excluded Locked

Most of the time you probably don't need to set all of these as some of them are rarely used.

Once we have set all the background and foreground colors, we can then assign the `UserPreference` object as the user preferences for the current user. This causes the options to be written to the user's `Settings.ini` file in `C:\Users\username\AppData\Roaming\QlikTech\QlikView`.

It is worth noting that multiple users in an organization should not use multiple different colors for selections, and so on. This could cause a lot of confusion!

There's more...

The API gives us access to a lot of settings like this, which have no UI to allow them to be set otherwise.

By default, QlikView installs a `PDF` and a very useful `QVW` file, that fully documents the API functionality, in `C:\ProgramData\QlikTech\QlikView Documentation\Automation`.

See also

▶ The *Changing the default selection color scheme* recipe
▶ The *Modifying the green, white and gray selection color schemes on QlikView Server* recipe

Modifying the green, white, and gray selection color schemes in QlikView Server

In the previous recipe, *Modifying the green, white, and gray selection color schemes*, we used the API to modify a user's default color scheme. However, this is a user setting and doesn't automatically apply to QlikView Server.

In this recipe, we will take the setting generated in the last recipe and apply them manually to QlikView Server.

Getting ready

Complete the previous recipe, *Modifying the green, white and gray selection color schemes*.

How to do it...

These steps show you how to modify the green, white, and gray color scheme on QlikView Server:

1. Locate your `Settings.ini` file in `C:\Users\username\AppData\Roaming\QlikTech\QlikView`.

2. Open the file in Notepad and locate the `CustSel` entries. Select them all and copy them to the clipboard (*Ctrl + C*).

3. On the QlikView Server, stop the QlikView Server Service.

4. Locate the `Settings.ini` file in `C:\ProgramData\QlikTech\QlikViewServer`.

5. Paste the `CustSel` values from the user `Settings.ini` file at the bottom of the `[Settings 7]` section. Save the file and start the QlikView Server.

6. Either copy the test file from the previous recipe into one of the server document folders, or modify one of the existing server documents to have the `[Custom]` color scheme (see previous recipe).

7. Open the document in the browser and see if the new color scheme has been applied.

How it works...

Some of the user settings that are stored in local user folders can also be applied to the server. By manually moving the settings from the same section in the user's `Settings.ini` file into the server's `Settings.ini` file, we are enabling the custom color scheme.

See also

▶ The *Modifying the green, white, and gray selection color schemes* recipe

Using containers as an alternative to multiboxes

Multi Boxes have been around in QlikView for a long time. They can be a useful way of adding many selectors to the layout when there is little room for a lot of listboxes.

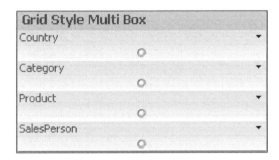

They can be presented either in the default, lateral mode, with the drop-down list across from the label, or in **Grid Mode**, with the drop-down list underneath the label.

I used Multi Boxes for many years and quite liked the **Grid Mode** style. However, there was a major problem. Unfortunately, the **Grid Mode** style is not supported in the AJAX ZFC web client.

Since Version 10 of QlikView, I have moved away from Multi Boxes and instead use a container control with listboxes. I believe that it is a much better way of accessing many fields in a small form factor.

Getting ready

Load the following script:

```
LOAD * INLINE [
    Country, Product, SalesPerson, Category, Sales
    USA, Widget, Joe, Widgets, 1234
    USA, Woggle, Joe, Widgets, 1983
    USA, Brogue, Jane, Footwear, 1175
    USA, Clog, Jane, Footwear, 1376
```

```
        UK,  Widget,  Tom,  Widgets,  954
        UK,  Woggle,  Tom,  Widgets,  953
        UK,  Brogue,  Tom,  Footwear,  989
        UK,  Clog,  Tom,  Footwear,  875
        Japan,  Widget,  Mike,  Widgets,  1265
        Japan,  Woggle,  Mike,  Widgets,  1345
        Japan,  Brogue,  Jane,  Footwear,  1425
        Japan,  Clog,  Jane,  Footwear,  1324
   ];
```

How to do it...

To implement a container as an alternative to a Multi Box, follow these steps:

1. Add listboxes to the layout for the four dimensions – **Country**, **Category**, **Product**, and **SalesPerson**.

2. Add a `Container` object to the layout. Don't add any objects using the **Properties** dialog, and just click on **OK**.

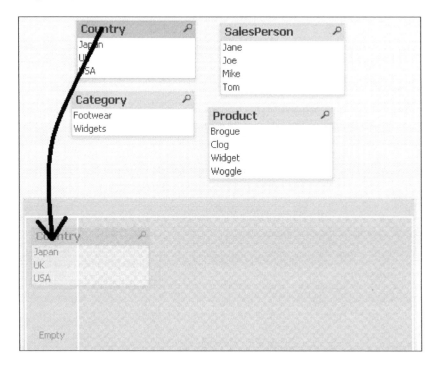

3. Drag each of the listboxes into the container.

4. Edit the properties of the container. On the **Presentation** tab, change the **Appearance** to **Tabs to the right**.

5. On the **Caption** tab, set the **Title Text** to **Selections**.

How it works...

Containers are a really useful type of object because they can contain any other object, including other containers.

Many people have seen them used to display several charts, but forget other possible uses such as this one. I pretty much use this for every QlikView document that I create.

Using the design menus to custom format a cell

There are two design menus that can appear when you right-click an object on the layout. They are:

▸ **Order**: This is applicable to all objects, and this menu has a submenu that allows you to adjust the **Layer** of an object.

▸ **Custom Format Cells**: This is applicable only to the three grid objects (Table Box, Straight Table, and Pivot Table), and this menu allows you to apply your own custom color, border, and font options to a cell.

These menu items do not appear by default. There are two ways of making them available. You can either turn on the **Design Grid** option (from the **View** menu), or you can turn them on by changing your **User Preferences**, which we will do in this recipe.

Getting ready

Load the following script:

```
Load * Inline [
  Country, Sales, Costs
  USA, 1203, 1043
  UK, 987, 995
  France, 1118, 1022
  Germany, 876, 754
];
```

How to do it...

Use the following steps to custom format a cell in the table:

1. Create a straight table with **Country** as dimension and add the following three expressions:

Total Sales	Sum(Sales)
Total Costs	Sum(Costs)
Total Margin	[Total Sales]-[Total Costs]

2. Click on **Finish** to save the chart.

3. From the **Settings** menu, select **User Preferences** and click on the **Design** tab.

4. Click on the **Always Show Design Menu Items** option and click on **OK**.

5. Right-click on one of the **Total Margin** values for a country (for example, 160 for USA) and select **Custom Format Cell** from the menu.

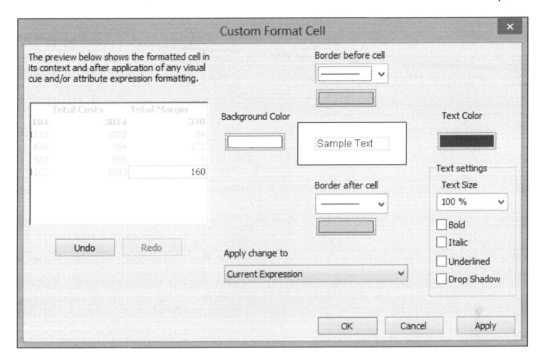

6. Click on the **Background Color** button and change the **Base Color, Fixed** to an RGB value of 245, 245, and 245. Set the **Apply change to** option to **Current Expression** and click on **OK**.

7. Right-click on the total value for **Total Margin** (in this case, 370) and select **Custom Format Cell**. Set the **Text Size** to **120 %** and turn on the **Italic** checkbox. Click on **OK** to make the change.

8. Similarly, right-click on one of the countries (for example, **Germany**) and select **Custom Format Cell**. Turn on the **Bold** option and click on **OK**:

Total Sales			
Country	Total Sales	Total Costs	Total Margin
	4184	3814	*370*
France	1118	1022	96
Germany	876	754	122
UK	987	995	-8
USA	1203	1043	160

9. Edit the properties of the chart and go to the **Style** tab. Note that the **Current Style** is set to **[Custom]**.

How it works...

This is quite simple, turning on the option in the **User Preferences** allows us to see the menu and that then allows us to make custom format changes to our tabular chart.

There's more...

If you change the **Current Style** option in the chart properties to one of the preset styles, it will remove all your custom settings.

3
Set Analysis

In this chapter, we will cover the following recipes:

- ▸ Using dollar expansion in Set Analysis to enable from-date and to-date selection
- ▸ Using alternate states with Set Analysis
- ▸ Using Set operators to exclude values from results
- ▸ Using Set Analysis with a Date Island
- ▸ Using Sets to avoid key tables

Introduction

I was lucky enough to attend the 2008 QlikView Global Partner Conference, Qonnections, in the Loews Hotel, Miami Beach.

There were several significant things that happened at that event, including a key note speech from Stephen Few and Capricorn Ventis winning a partner award.

From a technical point of view, the most significant thing that happened was during the CTO's report—Jonas Nachmanson announced the forthcoming Set Analysis in QlikView 8.5. When Jonas was done, all of the techies in the room gave a standing ovation. It was pretty incredible.

Prior to version 8.5, if I wanted to calculate the sales for the current year, I had to do something like this:

```
Sum(If(Year=vMaxYear, Sales, 0))
```

If the user then clicked on a different year, the values changed.

Now, I can write it as follows:

```
Sum({<Year={$(=Max({1} Year))}>} Sales)
```

The syntax is a little arcane, but easy once you become experienced with it.

If the user changes the selection, it doesn't matter, because the year is going to be static. There are so many ways that this can be useful. Being able to get access to values that are excluded by selection gives us a huge amount of flexibility. I could now do things that I could never have dreamed of in version 8.2.

In my opinion, Set Analysis is the most significant technical addition to the product since it added 64-bit ability.

Using dollar expansion in Set Analysis to enable from-date and to-date selection

Set Analysis is enormously versatile and useful for QlikView developers. A lot of the versatility comes from being able to use dynamically calculated values.

Prior to the introduction of Set Analysis in version 8.5, the only way that we could use any type of dynamic value was by assigning an expression to a variable and then using that variable. In 8.5, QlikView introduced a new way of doing that—**Dollar Expansion**.

In this recipe, we are going to allow the user to specify a "from date" and a "to date", and then click on a button to make the selection. Since this is functionality that is available in many reporting tools, it can help some users get into QlikView.

Getting ready

Load the following script:

```
LOAD * INLINE [
  Country, Value, SalesDate
  USA, 12, 2013-01-04
  USA, 14.5, 2013-02-07
  USA, 6.6, 2013-03-03
  USA, 4.5, 2013-04-11
  USA, 7.8, 2013-05-19
  USA, 9.4, 2013-06-22
  UK, 11.3, 2013-01-31
  UK, 10.1, 2013-02-01
  UK, 3.2, 2013-03-21
```

```
   UK, 5.6, 2013-04-15
   UK, 3.9, 2013-05-12
   UK, 6.9, 2013-06-06
];

Let vFromDate=Floor(Date#('2013-01-01', 'YYYY-MM-DD'));
Let vToDate=Floor(Date#('2013-06-30', 'YYYY-MM-DD'));
```

How to do it...

Perform the following steps to use dollar expansion in Set Analysis:

1. Create a `Slider/Calendar` object with **Input Style** set to **Calendar**. The **Data** option should be **Variable(s)**, and the variable **vFromDate** should be selected.

2. Note that it is very important that no **Min Value** or **Max Value** are specified, as these will restrict the minimum and maximum dates selectable by the calendar control.

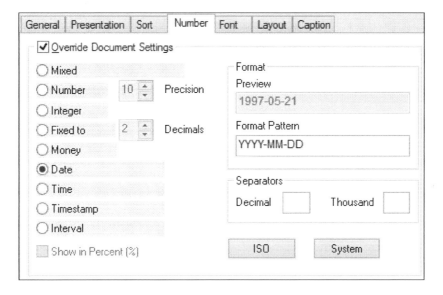

3. On the **Number** tab, override the document settings and select a date format with **Format Pattern** set to **YYYY-MM-DD**.

4. On the **Caption** tab, enable the **Show Caption** option and enter `From Date` as the **Title Text**. Click on **OK**.

5. Add another `Calendar` object for the **vToDate** variable with the same **Number** properties. Enter **To Date** for the caption.

6. Create a new bar chart with `SalesDate` as dimension. Add the following expression:

```
Sum({$<SalesDate={
'>=$(=Date(vFromDate, 'YYYY-MM-DD'))<=$(=Date(vToDate, 'YYYY-MM-
DD'))'
}>} Value)
```

Note that the preceding code text wraps because of the page size; it should not when you type it in the expression editor.

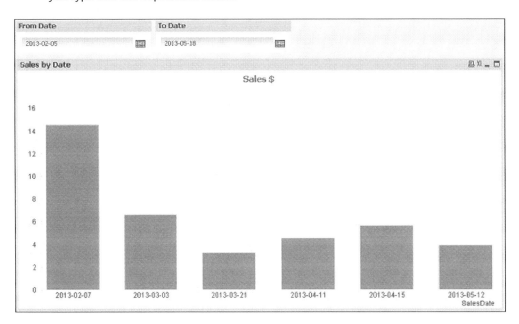

7. Note what happens when you make different date selections in the calendar control.

How it works...

The first thing to understand is the creation of the variables in the script:

```
Let vFromDate=Floor(Date#('2013-01-01', 'YYYY-MM-DD'));
Let vToDate=Floor(Date#('2013-06-30', 'YYYY-MM-DD'));
```

Under the hood, dates in QlikView are stored as numbers. This syntax ensures that the correct serial integer is assigned to each variable to represent an initial start and end date.

The reason that I did this is because that is what the `Calendar` object in QlikView does—it will assign a number, representing the selected date, to the variable. In general, it is always better to have a date represented as a number for calculation and comparison.

When we create the `Calendar` objects, we assign a format string so that the user doesn't have to deal with the underlying number.

There are two Dollar Expansions in the set expression:

```
$(=Date(vFromDate, 'YYYY-MM-DD'))
```

And

```
$(=Date(vToDate, 'YYYY-MM-DD'))
```

Both of these simply apply a format to the relevant variable, so that it is run as if the developer had typed the value from the variable into the set:

```
Sum({<SalesDate={
'>=2013-02-05<=2013-05-18'
}>} Value)
```

Using alternate states with Set Analysis

The alternate states function was introduced to QlikView in version 11. It allows us to create a named set of selections separate to the default current selections. At a simple level, this allows us to create a side-by-side analysis to allow us to easily and quickly compare one set of selections versus another. At a more complex level, it opens up a wide range of analysis possibilities.

In this recipe, we will create two states and look at how we access those states in the Set Analysis syntax.

Getting ready

Load the following script:

```
LOAD * INLINE [
  Country, City, Year, Sales
  USA, San Francisco, 2011, 1245
  USA, San Francisco, 2012, 3322
  USA, San Francisco, 2013, 3245
  USA, New York, 2011, 2765
  USA, New York, 2012, 3452
  USA, New York, 2013, 3321
  UK, London, 2011, 2765
  UK, London, 2012, 2612
  UK, London, 2013, 1498
```

```
    UK, Manchester, 2011, 1654
    UK, Manchester, 2012, 3522
    UK, Manchester, 2013, 4865
];
```

How to do it...

Perform the following steps to use alternate states with Set Analysis:

1. Add listboxes onto the layout for **Country**, **City**, and **Year**.

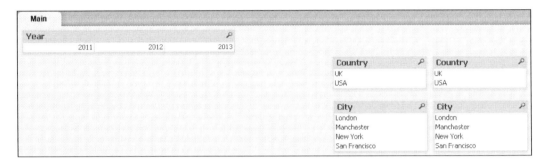

2. Make a copy of the **Country** and **City** listboxes.

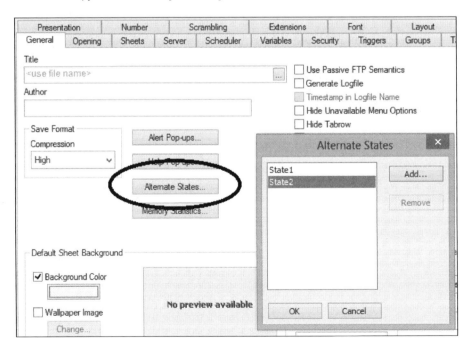

3. From the **Settings** menu, select **Document Properties**. On the **General** tab, click on **Alternate States....** On the **Alternate States** dialog box, click on **Add** and enter a new state called `State1`. Repeat and add a state called `State2`.

4. Click on **OK**. Close **Document Properties**.

5. Edit the properties for the first **Country** listbox. Set the **Title** to **Country – State 1**. Select **State1** from the **Alternate State** drop-down list. Click on **OK**.

6. Set the properties for the other three listboxes, as follows:

Listbox	Title	Alternate State
City	City – State 1	State1
Country 2	Country – State 2	State2
City 2	City – State 2	State2

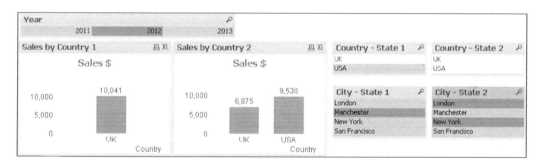

7. Add a new bar chart with **Country** as dimension and **Sum(Sales)** as an expression. Set **Alternate State** to **State1**. Copy this chart and set **Alternate State** of the copy to **State2**.

8. Note how the different selections in different listboxes change the results displayed in the different charts. However, the **Year** listbox does not change the results in either chart.

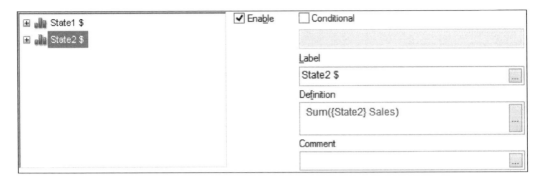

9. Add a new bar chart. This time, there is no dimension. Add the following two expressions:

State1 $	Sum({State1} Sales)
State2 $	Sum({State2} Sales)

10. Make a copy of this chart and change the expressions as follows:

State1 $	Sum({State1<Year=P({$} Year)>} Sales)
State2 $	Sum({State2<Year=P({$} Year)>} Sales)

11. Note what happens when different selections are made; especially in **Year**.

How it works...

The first two charts are in different states and only react to the selections from the other listboxes that are in the same state; they don't react to changes in the **Year** list as it is in the default, `<inherited>`, state.

The third chart is in the default state but because the expressions have the Set syntax with the state names, they still only react to the listboxes in those states.

Finally, we add an implicit Set identifier to the default set (`{$}`), so that selections in the **Year** listbox now make changes to the values in the chart.

There's more...

If an object is not assigned to a particular state, it will default to inheriting the state of its parent. That parent could be a container object or a sheet, either of which can have a different state assigned to it. Unless a different state is assigned to a sheet, the sheet inherits the default selections of the document.

There are many potential uses for alternate states, especially when combined with Set syntax. For example, traditional **Date Islands** could be replaced with a state. However, you should be careful that any use of states should not confuse the user as to what they are selecting. A careful use of legends, colors, or textboxes should be applied to make sure that they know what they are looking at.

An interesting thing to note here is that anything you type into a search expression in a listbox is a valid option for a Set modifier expression.

This is an important consideration when dealing with dual values, such as dates and money. In the preceding example, we have used a `Date` function to format the variable to the same format as is used by the `SalesDate` field. This isn't entirely necessary, but I find it useful to do so; just to be sure.

To explain why, let us look at an example. In our dataset there is a `SalesDate` value representing 1st February, 2013. This is a dual value that has the following two values:

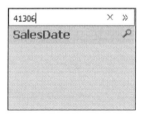

If I were to search for `41306` in a listbox containing `SalesDate`, I would get no matches.

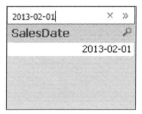

If I search using the text value, I get an output.

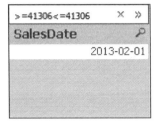

Interestingly, if I use a >= and <= syntax, using just the one value, I do get an output!

The same rule applies in the set syntax:

```
Sum({<SalesDate={'2013-02-01'}>} Value)
```

This will return a value, but look at these two:

```
Sum({<SalesDate={41306}>} Value)
```

Or

```
Sum({<SalesDate={'41306'}>} Value)
```

Both of these tests are valid syntactically, but neither will return a value.

If we change the later one to use >= and <= of the same value:

```
Sum({<SalesDate={'>=41306<=41306'}>} Value)
```

This will work!

Since this can be somewhat confusing, I will try and stick to using the text value of a dual all the time, as follows:

```
Sum({<SalesDate={'>=2013-02-05<=2013-05-18'}>} Value)
```

Instead of this:

```
Sum({<SalesDate={'>=41310<=41412'}>} Value)
```

See Also

▶   The *Using Set Analysis with a Date Island* recipe in this chapter

Using Set operators to exclude values from results

Many people who start using Set Analysis will learn how to include values that they want in the results using modifiers. However, it is not always easy to work out how to exclude values. This recipe will show you how to do it.

Getting ready

Load the following script:

```
LOAD * INLINE [
   Country, Year, Sales
   USA, 2011, 4322
   USA, 2012, 5322
   USA, 2013, 6521
   UK, 2011, 1985
   UK, 2012, 2319
   UK, 2013, 3211
];
```

How to do it...

Perform the following steps to exclude the values from the results using Set operators:

1. Add a straight table with **Country** as dimension. Add the following expressions:

Sales $	Sum(Sales)
Sales ex. 2013	Sum({<Year=-{2013}>} Sales)
Sales less 2013	Sum({<Year-={2013}>} Sales)

The syntax highlight may suggest that these are incorrect; they are not!

2. Add a listbox for **Year**.

Sales $				Year	
Country	Sales $	Sales ex. 2013	Sales less 2013		2011
	23680	13948	13948		2012
UK	7515	4304	4304		2013
USA	16165	9644	9644		

3. Notice the values with no selections on. Both of the values excluding **2013** appear to be the same. Select **2012** in the listbox:

Sales $			🖳 XL ▁ ☐	Year	🔎
Country	⟍ Sales $	Sales ex. 2013	Sales less 2013		2011
	7641	**13948**	**7641**		2012
UK	2319	4304	2319		2013
USA	5322	9644	5322		

4. Note that **Sales ex. 2013** didn't change. **Sales less 2013** now matches the **Sales $**. Select **2013** in the listbox:

Sales $			🖳 XL ▁ ☐	Year	🔎
Country	⟍ Sales $	Sales ex. 2013	Sales less 2013		2011
	9732	**13948**	**0**		2012
UK	3211	4304	0		2013
USA	6521	9644	0		

5. Again, **Sales ex. 2013** didn't change. **Sales less 2013** is zero.

How it works...

The difference is on which side of "=" we add the "-" sign. The first Set expression looks similar to the following:

```
Sum({<Year=-{2013}>} Sales)
```

This is actually syntactically the same as this (and this is a valid syntax):

```
Sum({<Year={*}-{2013}>} Sales)
```

{*} here means all possible values of the year.

This Set syntax will always override the selection on `Year`, so it will not change when we choose a different year. The result stays the same.

The second Set expression looks similar to the following:

```
Sum({<Year-={2013}>} Sales)
```

This is actually and "additive" (or, in this case, "subtractive") way of writing the Set syntax. It is syntactically the same as follows:

```
Sum({<Year=Year-{2013}>} Sales)
```

So `Year` is "Year less 2013". So, it will match whatever value we select for the year, except for 2013. This syntax will be familiar to anyone who is used to writing C or Java code.

There's more...

It is also possible to use "+" instead of "-" to force the inclusion of a value in a Set:

```
Sum({<Year+={2013}>} Sales)
```

In this case, `2013` will always be included, no matter what other values are selected.

Using Set Analysis with a Date Island

It is not uncommon to create a "Date Island"—a disconnected calendar table—in the data. Users make selections on the island values and then these values are used in the Set syntax to limit the results.

Getting ready

Load the following script:

```
// Load Transactions
Transactions:
LOAD * INLINE [
  TransDate, TransType, TransValue
  2012-01-12, Sale, 100
  2012-02-01, Sale, 100
  2012-03-05, Sale, 100
  2012-03-31, Payment, 200
  2012-04-29, Sale, 150
  2012-05-19, Sale, 175
  2012-06-02, Sale, 200
  2012-06-30, Payment, 400
  2012-07-03, Sale, 200
  2012-08-13, Sale, 100
  2012-09-22, Sale, 200
  2012-09-30, Payment, 400
  2012-10-10, Sale, 175
  2012-11-14, Sale, 225
  2012-12-02, Sale, 325
  2012-12-31, Payment, 400
];
```

```
// Load the Date Island
Let vStartDate=Floor(MakeDate(2012));
Let vEndDate=Floor(MakeDate(2012,12,31));
Let vDiff=vEndDate-vStartDate+1;

DateIsland:
Load
    TempDate as DateID,
    Year(TempDate) As Year,
    Month(TempDate) As Month;
Load
    $(vStartDate)+RecNo()-1 As TempDate
AutoGenerate($(vDiff));
```

How to do it...

Perform the following steps to use Set Analysis with a Date Island:

1. Add a new PIVOT TABLE. Do not add a dimension. Add the following expressions:

Sales	Sum({<TransType={'Sale'}>} TransValue)
Payments	Sum({<TransType={'Payment'}>} TransValue)
Balance	Sum({<TransType={'Sale'}>} TransValue) - Sum({<TransType={'Payment'}>} TransValue)
Sales in Period	Sum({< TransType={'Sale'}, TransDate={">=$(=Min(DateID))<=$(=Max(DateID))"} >} TransValue)
Payments in Period	Sum({< TransType={'Payment'}, TransDate={">=$(=Min(DateID))<=$(=Max(DateID))"} >} TransValue)
Balance in Period	Sum({< TransType={'Sale'}, TransDate={">=$(=Min(DateID))<=$(=Max(DateID))"} >} TransValue) - Sum({< TransType={'Payment'}, TransDate={">=$(=Min(DateID))<=$(=Max(DateID))"} >} TransValue)

Sales to Date	```Sum({<```
	```TransType={'Sale'},```
	```TransDate={"<=$(=Max(DateID))"}```
	```>} TransValue)```

Payments to Date	```Sum({<```
	```TransType={'Payment'},```
	```TransDate={"<=$(=Max(DateID))"}```
	```>} TransValue)```

Balance to Date	```Sum({<```
	```TransType={'Sale'},```
	```TransDate={"<=$(=Max(DateID))"}```
	```>} TransValue)-```
	```Sum({<```
	```TransType={'Payment'},```
	```TransDate={"<=$(=Max(DateID))"}```
	```>} TransValue)```

2. Add a listbox for **Month** onto the layout.

Sales		囻 XL ＿ ☐	Month	🔍
				Jan
Sales		2050		Feb
Payments		1400		Mar
Balance		650		Apr
Sales in Period		500		May
Payments in Period		400		Jun
Balance in Period		100		Jul
Sales to Date		1325		Aug
Payments to Date		1000		Sep
Balance to Date		325		Oct
				Nov
				Dec

3. Note the values that calculate with different selections.

How it works...

The disconnected dataset gives us the confidence that any selection on **Month** is going to give us the correct start and end `DateID` values; there is no possibility of interference from any other selection (for example, a product that has not been sold in a period).

Once we have that, we can establish both the beginning and end dates for the selection, and feed those values into a Set expression using dollar expansion.

There's more...

This could also be achieved with a connected calendar table using Alternate State.

See Also

▶   The *Using Alternate States with Set Analysis* recipe in this chapter

Using Sets to avoid key tables

Key tables are used to associate data where those associations can be quite complex. They sometimes can be quite awkward to build and difficult to maintain. It can be useful to have a strategy to avoid using them, especially if you need to get something delivered quickly.

Here, we will learn how to use an implicit set to achieve this.

Getting ready

Load the following script:

```
// Load some sales
Sales:
Load * INLINE [
Date, Item, Store, Quantity, Price, NetValue
2009-01-01, 1, 1, 1, 2.00, 2.00
2009-01-01, 1, 2, 2, 2.00, 4.00
2009-01-01, 2, 1, 1, 2.00, 2.00
2009-02-01, 2, 2, 1, 3.00, 3.00
2009-02-01, 1, 1, 3, 3.00, 9.00
2009-02-01, 2, 2, 1, 3.00, 3.00
];
```

```
// Load the products
Product:
Load * INLINE [
Item, Description
1, Product A
2, Product B
];

// Load the stores
Store:
Load * INLINE [
Store, Name
1, Store 1A
2, Store 2B
] ;

// Load stock
Stock:
Load * INLINE [
StockStore, Item, OnHand
1, 1, 55
1, 2, 33
2, 1, 23
2, 2, 12
];
```

How to do it...

Perform the following steps to avoid a key table by using Sets:

1. Add a straight table with **Description** as the dimension.

2. Add the following expressions:

Incorrect On Hand	Sum (OnHand)
Correct On Hand	Sum({<StockStore = P({$} Store)>} OnHand)

Incorrect On Hand			Name	
Description	**Incorrect On H...**	**Correct On Hand**	Store 1A	
	123	123	Store 2B	
Product A	78	78		
Product B	45	45		

3. Add a listbox for **Name**.

Incorrect On Hand			Name
Description	**Incorrect On H..**	**Correct On Hand**	Store 1A
	123	**88**	Store 2B
Product A	78	55	
Product B	45	33	

4. Select a store and note the results.

How it works...

In this load, we have loaded the Stock table's `StoreID` as `StockStore`. This was to avoid the dreaded synthetic key.

The first expression doesn't work correctly because the `Stock` table is not now connected directly to the store. The implicit set, `P()`, returns all the possible values of the `Store` field. By using this implicit set against the `StockStore` field, we get the correct answer.

There's more...

This section just shows that you will not always have to connect all of the data. It is possible to connect the data in expressions using the implicit Set syntax. However, it should be noted that performance should be better with a well-designed data model.

4

Advanced Aggregations

In this chapter, we will cover the following recipes:

- ▸ Using TOTAL to calculate the percentage of total and the percentage of subtotal
- ▸ Using AGGR to calculate the percentage of the maximum value
- ▸ Using AGGR to resolve a "Sum of Rows" issue
- ▸ Creating a dynamic AGGR expression for a Group dimension using Dollar Expansion
- ▸ Using RangeMax to return only positive numbers
- ▸ Creating a dynamic Part-to-Whole pie chart
- ▸ Creating a colored treemap using colormix
- ▸ Using RangeSum to calculate a rolling total in a multi-dimension table
- ▸ Showing only the top 3 values in a pivot table
- ▸ Creating a Statistical Control Chart using Standard Deviation
- ▸ Creating a Moving Range chart
- ▸ Creating a Control Chart using Moving Range

Introduction

Simple, straightforward aggregation functions are the staple of QlikView. Nine times out of ten, we tend to use something like `Sum()`, `Count()`, or `Avg()`. We might add in some Set Analysis, but the basic function is the same.

We usually call these "horizontal" functions, because they are calculated on the row, in the chart for the dimension on that row. So, we calculate the sum of sales for each country, or we count the number of purchase orders for each year.

From time-to-time, we need to break out of the row and perform "vertical" calculations. For these, we need to look at more advanced aggregation functions using TOTAL, AGGR, or one of the range functions.

Using TOTAL to calculate the percentage of total and subtotal

TOTAL is a useful qualifier that can be added to an aggregation function (such as Sum, Count, and Avg) to tell QlikView to ignore the dimensions of a chart in the calculation. By default, it ignores all the dimensions, but we can be more specific and tell it to ignore some while respecting others.

In this recipe, we will calculate the percentage of total sales for each city, as well as the percentage of sales for each city within its own country.

Getting ready

Load the following script:

```
LOAD * INLINE [
    Country, City, Sales
    USA, San Diego, 24567
    USA, Dallas, 54962
    USA, New York, 67013
    USA, Boston, 45824
    UK, London, 64002
    UK, Birmingham, 44291
    UK, Manchester, 40320
    Germany, Berlin, 52912
    Germany, Frankfurt, 61832
    Germany, Munich, 35812
    Japan, Tokyo, 42137
    Japan, Yokohama, 55832
    Japan, Osaka, 37643
];
```

How to do it...

The following steps show how to use TOTAL to calculate the percentage of total and the percentage of subtotal:

1. Create a new pivot table with **Country** and **City** as dimensions.

2. Add the following expressions:

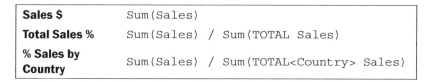

Sales $	Sum(Sales)
Total Sales %	Sum(Sales) / Sum(TOTAL Sales)
% Sales by Country	Sum(Sales) / Sum(TOTAL<Country> Sales)

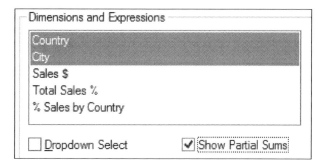

3. On the **Presentation** tab, select the **Country** and **City** dimensions and turn on **Show Partial Sums**.

4. On the **Number** tab, set the format for the first expression to **Integer**. Set the second and third expression to **Fixed to 2** decimals, and turn on **Show in Percent (%)**.

5. Click on **Finish** to save the chart.

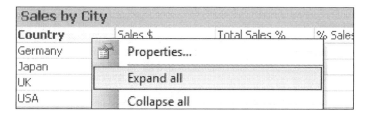

6. Right-click on the **Country** field in the pivot table, and select **Expand all** from the menu to show all the cities:

Country	City	Sales $	Total Sales %	% Sales by Coun...
	⊟ Berlin	52,912	8.44%	35.14%
	Frankfurt	61,832	9.86%	41.07%
Germany	Munich	35,812	5.71%	23.79%
	Total	**150,556**	**24.01%**	**100.00%**
	⊟ Osaka	37,643	6.00%	27.76%
	Tokyo	42,137	6.72%	31.07%
Japan	Yokohama	55,832	8.90%	41.17%
	Total	**135,612**	**21.62%**	**100.00%**
	⊟ Birmingham	44,291	7.06%	29.80%
	London	64,002	10.21%	43.07%
UK	Manchester	40,320	6.43%	27.13%
	Total	**148,613**	**23.70%**	**100.00%**
	⊟ Boston	45,824	7.31%	23.82%
	Dallas	54,962	8.76%	28.57%
USA	New York	67,013	10.69%	34.84%
	San Diego	24,567	3.92%	12.77%
	Total	**192,366**	**30.67%**	**100.00%**
Total		**627,147**	**100.00%**	**100.00%**

Sales by City

7. Resize the chart to see all of the values.

How it works...

In the first expression, the TOTAL syntax instructs that part of the expression to ignore the dimensions of the chart, and calculate the sum across the whole chart. The calculated percentage is the sales over the overall total (627,147).

In the second expression, the syntax is TOTAL<Country>. This tells that part of the expression to ignore all the dimensions; except **Country**. This gives us a subtotal by each country, and the calculated percentage is the percentage sales for that city within its own country.

There's more...

Within other charts, there is another way to achieve the overall total and that is to turn on the **Relative** checkbox against the expression. This option is not available in pivot tables.

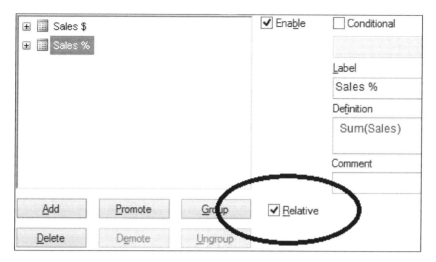

Using AGGR to calculate the percentage of the maximum value

AGGR is the function that we will use to perform vertical calculations.

In this case, we are going to work out which country has the highest value, and calculate the percentage of other sales versus that highest value.

Getting ready

Load the following script:

```
LOAD * INLINE [
  Country, City, Sales
  USA, San Diego, 24567
  USA, Dallas, 54962
  USA, New York, 67013
  USA, Boston, 45824
  UK, London, 64002
  UK, Birmingham, 44291
  UK, Manchester, 40320
  Germany, Berlin, 52912
  Germany, Frankfurt, 61832
  Germany, Munich, 35812
  Japan, Tokyo, 42137
```

```
    Japan, Yokohama, 55832
    Japan, Osaka, 37643
];
```

How to do it...

Use the following steps to use AGGR to calculate the percentage of the maximum:

1. Create a new straight table with **Country** and **City** as dimensions.

2. Add the following expressions:

Sales $	Sum(Sales)
% of Max	Sum(Sales) / Max(TOTAL Aggr(Sum(Sales), Country, City))

3. On the **Expression** tab, for the second expression, under **Total Mode**, select **No Total**.

4. On the **Number** tab, set the format for the first expression to **Integer**. Set the second expression to **Fixed to 2 decimals**, and turn on **Show in Percent (%)**.

5. Click on **Finish** to save the chart.

Sales by City			믐 XL ▬ ☐
Country	**City**	**Sales $**	**% of Max**
		627,147	
USA	San Diego	24,567	36.66%
Germany	Munich	35,812	53.44%
Japan	Osaka	37,643	56.17%
UK	Manchester	40,320	60.17%
Japan	Tokyo	42,137	62.88%
UK	Birmingham	44,291	66.09%
USA	Boston	45,824	68.38%
Germany	Berlin	52,912	78.96%
USA	Dallas	54,962	82.02%
Japan	Yokohama	55,832	83.32%
Germany	Frankfurt	61,832	92.27%
UK	London	64,002	95.51%
USA	New York	67,013	100.00%

6. Double-click on the **% of Max** label to sort the values.

How it works...

There are a couple of things going on here. First, the AGGR expression:

```
Aggr(Sum(Sales), Country, City)
```

AGGR basically creates a table chart in the memory. In this case, the expression is Sum (Sales), and there are two dimensions—**Country** and **City**.

Country	City	
USA	San Diego	24,567
Germany	Munich	35,812
Japan	Osaka	37,643
UK	Manchester	40,320
Japan	Tokyo	42,137
UK	Birmingham	44,291
USA	Boston	45,824
Germany	Berlin	52,912
USA	Dallas	54,962
Japan	Yokohama	55,832
Germany	Frankfurt	61,832
UK	London	
USA	New York	67,013

Once we have this in-memory chart, we can put one of our many aggregation functions (such as Sum, Min, Max, and Stdev) around it to get a result. In this case, we use the Max function to retrieve the maximum value in the range (67,013).

Since we are using the function in a chart that has dimensions, we also need to include the TOTAL qualifier to tell the Max expression to ignore the dimensions. If we didn't, we would just get 100 percent for every row!

There's more...

This is a relatively basic use of AGGR, but it actually doesn't get much more complicated! When you add in the Set Analysis syntax into an expression, you can then finely control the range of values that are returned.

Just remember that AGGR is an in-memory chart. Like all charts, it has an expression and one or many dimensions. If you can build a straight table to get the result you are looking for, then you can build an AGGR statement.

Any time that you find yourself writing an expression that has one aggregation function nested inside another—like `Max(Sum(Sales))`—then you will need to use AGGR to have the function calculate as expected—like `Max(Aggr(Sum(Sales), Country))`.

Using AGGR to resolve a "Sum of Rows" issue

"Sum of Rows" issues are reasonably rare. Essentially, what it means is that the sum that is displayed as the total on a table is not actually the sum of the rows displayed in the table (usually discovered when exporting to Excel), or the total is not calculated at all. Often, it can be the result of a complicated `if` statement in the expression, or from using values from across different tables in the expression.

In this recipe, we will look at a very simple example and see how to resolve it using AGGR.

Getting ready

Load the following script:

```
// Load Sales data
Sales:
LOAD * INLINE [
    Country, Month, Curr, ProdID, Price, Qty
    USA, 2013-01-01, USD, 1, 1.99, 2
    USA, 2013-02-01, USD, 2, 2.99, 3
    USA, 2013-03-01, USD, 1, 1.98, 5
    UK, 2013-01-01, GBP, 1, 1.59, 1
    UK, 2013-02-01, GBP, 1, 1.58, 3
    UK, 2013-03-01, GBP, 1, 1.58, 3
    UK, 2013-03-01, GBP, 1, 1.58, 3
];

// Load Exchange Rates
LOAD * INLINE [
    Curr, ExRate
    USD, 1
    GBP, 0.63
];
```

How to do it...

These steps show how to resolve a "Sum of Rows" issue with AGGR:

1. Create a new straight table with **Country** as the dimension.
2. Add the following three expressions:

Volume	Sum(Qty)
Sales $	Sum(Price*Qty)/ExRate
Avg. Price	[Sales $] / Volume

3. Set the number format for the **Volume** expression to **Integer**. Set the format for the other two expressions to **Fixed to 2 Decimals**.
4. Click on **Finish** to save the chart.

Volume			
Country	**Volume**	**Sales $**	**Avg. Price**
	20 -	-	-
UK	10	25.10	2.51
USA	10	22.85	2.29

5. Note that the **Sales $ total** and **Avg. Price** values have not been calculated. Edit the properties of the chart and change the **Sales $** expression to the following:

```
Sum(AGGR(Sum(Price*Qty)/ExRate, Country))
```

Volume			
Country	**Volume**	**Sales $**	**Avg. Price**
	20	**47.95**	**2.40**
UK	10	25.10	2.51
USA	10	22.85	2.29

6. Note that the totals are now calculating.

How it works...

Initially, the total for **Sales $** does not work because the **ExRate** field will return more than one value at the total level, which invalidates the whole expression.

When we wrap the expression in the AGGR statement, it makes no difference at all at the line level—because the dimensions are being respected—but kicks in at the total level to give us the correct sum.

There's more...

It is useful to note that you can fix the sum of rows issue in a straight table by simply changing **Total Mode** of that expression to **Sum of Rows** instead of the default of **Expression Total**.

That method would not work though for the **Avg. Price** expression. Neither would it work in a pivot table, which does not have the option. AGGR will work great in the pivot table.

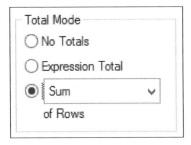

See also

▶ The *Creating a dynamic AGGR expression for a Group dimension using Dollar Expansion* recipe in this chapter

Creating a dynamic AGGR expression for a Group dimension using Dollar Expansion

AGGR is very useful for advanced aggregations. However, we need to be careful when using it in charts that have a Group dimension; either **cycle** or **drill**.

In this recipe, we will see how to overcome this using a Dollar Expansion.

Getting ready

This example follows along from the previous section. Load the data and create the straight table with the AGGR expression.

How to do it...

Follow these steps to create a dynamic AGGR expression for a group dimension:

1. In **Document Properties | Groups**, create a group called Cycle1 with **ProdID** and **Month** as the dimensions:

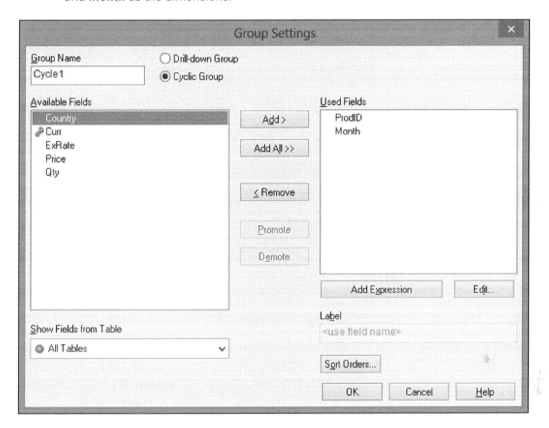

2. Edit the straight table and add Cycle1 as the second dimension.

3. Save the changes and look at the chart. Note that the expressions do not calculate correctly for all the different cycle values.

4. Open the properties of the table and edit the **Sales $** expression:

```
Sum(
AGGR(Sum(Price*Qty)/ExRate, Country,
[$(=GetCurrentField(Cycle1))])
)
```

5. Click on **OK** to save the chart:

Volume				
Country	ProdID	Volume	Sales $	Avg. Price
		20	47.95	2.40
USA	2	3	8.97	2.99
USA	1	7	13.88	1.98
UK	1	10	25.10	2.51

6. Click on the cycle button and confirm that the values calculate correctly.

How it works...

This is a great example of using Dollar Expansion in an expression when dealing with a Group dimension; or any other thing that might change.

When you click on the cycle button, the `GetCurrentField` function returns the name of the field that is now in use and that changes the field that the calculation is aggregating over. Note the use of square brackets around the Dollar Expansion; this is because any field in the cycle could potentially have a space or other character in the fieldname that could break the expression if the square brackets weren't there.

See also

▶ The *Using AGGR to resolve a "Sum of Rows" issue* recipe in this chapter

Using RangeMax to return only positive numbers

There are occasions where we need to only deal with positive values, such as when we have a chart that will not calculate with negative numbers or when an expression makes no sense having negative numbers.

In this case, we are going to display a block chart for sales, but deal with having negative values. A block chart does not calculate with negative numbers.

Getting ready

Load the following script:

```
LOAD * INLINE [
  Country, Sales
  USA, 120
  UK, 100
  Mexico, 76
  Canada, 32
  France, 10
  Germany, -5
];
```

How to do it...

The following steps show you how to use RangeMax to return only positive numbers:

1. Create a new block chart. Set **Country** as the dimension.

2. Add the following expression:

   Sum(Sales)

3. Click on **Finish** to save the chart:

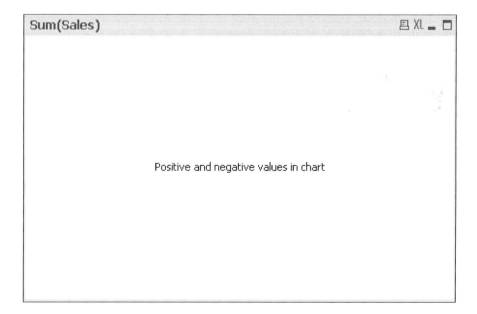

4. Edit the properties of the chart and change the expression to the following:

   ```
   RangeMax(Sum(Sales), 0)
   ```

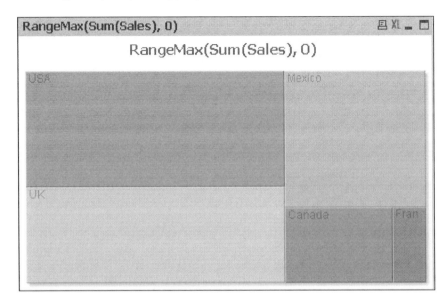

5. Confirm that the chart now displays the data. There should be no block for **Germany** as it was the negative value.

How it works...

The `RangeMax` function will return the highest value in the list of values. As long as `Sum(Sales)` is positive, it will always be higher than 0. Once it is negative, 0 will be returned by the function, and the negative value will not interfere with the calculation of the chart.

There's more...

Range functions are quite useful and work in both charts and scripts. They are essential when using functions such as `Above` and `Before`, which return a range of values.

See also

▶ The *Using RangeSum to calculate a rolling total in a table* recipe in this chapter

Creating a dynamic Part-to-Whole pie chart

Many visualization experts will argue over the merits of the humble pie chart. Most, however, will agree that the following example, with many segments, is probably the least useful implementation.

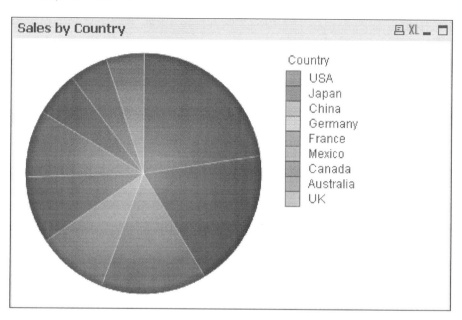

Pie charts are most useful when doing a simple part-to-whole comparison. In this recipe, we will create a dynamic part-to-whole bar chart that displays the sales value for the currently selected set of countries versus the rest.

Getting ready

Load the following script:

```
LOAD * INLINE [
   Country, Sales
   USA, 53453
   Mexico, 21317
   Canada, 14545
   UK, 12333
```

```
    France, 21333
    Germany, 23123
    Japan, 44342
    China, 34234
    Australia, 12345
];
```

How to do it...

To create a dynamic part-to-whole pie chart, follow these steps:

1. Create a new pie chart.

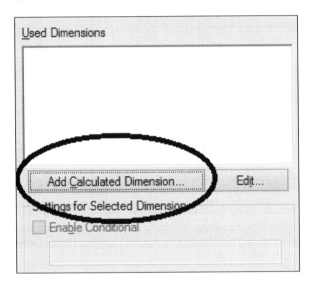

2. On the **Dimensions** tab, use the **Add Calculated Dimension** button to add the following dimension expression:

```
=if(
        Aggr(Sum(1), Country)>0,
        'Selected: $(=Concat(DISTINCT Country, ', '))',
        'Others: $(=Concat({<Country=E({$})>} DISTINCT Country, ',
'))'
    )
```

3. Label the dimension as Country.

4. Add the following expression:

   ```
   Sum({<Country=>} Sales)
   ```

5. Label the expression as `Sales $`.

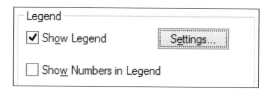

6. Click on **Next** until you get to the **Presentation** tab. Click on the **Settings** button for **Legend**:

7. Turn on the **Wrap Text** option and set **Cell Height** to 6. Click on **OK**. Finish the chart wizard.

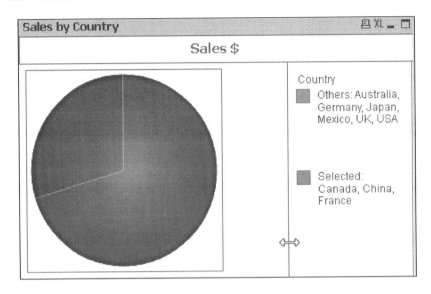

8. With the chart selected, hold down the *Ctrl + Shift* key. The different areas of the chart will be highlighted. Use the mouse to narrow the legend area.

9. Add a **Country** listbox to the layout, to the right of the pie chart. Note what happens as you make different selections.

How it works...

This is a great example of using an AGGR function in a calculated dimension to return just the dimension values that are of interest. In this case:

```
Aggr(Sum(1), Country)
```

Will only evaluate for those countries that are currently selected because Sum(1) will be null for the unselected countries. We check whether it is greater than 0 or not, and then use that as the list of selected countries (achieved using Concat).

The tricky bit is getting back the list of unselected countries. We can do that by using a Set:

```
Concat({<Country=E({$})>} DISTINCT Country, ', ')
```

The E() set returns the list of excluded values.

By putting the Concat functions inside a dollar expansion, we cause them to be evaluated separately to the chart, so they are calculated at the document level.

There's more...

Other functions can be used quite effectively within an AGGR like this. For example:

```
=if(
Aggr(Rank(Sum(Sales)), Country)<=3,
Country,
'Others'
)
```

This will give us back the top three countries by rank of `Sales`. A fourth value called `Others` will also appear in the dimensions.

See also

▸ The *Showing only the top three values in a pivot table* recipe in this chapter

Creating a colored treemap using colormix

Treemaps were originally designed by *Ben Shneiderman*, a professor of Computer Science at the University of Maryland. They are a very effective way of displaying hierarchical data. Within QlikView, the basic implementation of the Treemap, using the size of the rectangles to encode a value, can be effectively rendered by using the block chart.

If you want to encode a secondary measure, you can use a color function such as `colormix1`, along with an advanced aggregation statement.

In this recipe, we are going to compare sales values using the size of the rectangles and average order size using `color`.

Getting ready

Load the following script:

```
LOAD * INLINE [
  Country, City, Sales, Orders
  USA, San Diego, 24567, 546
  USA, Dallas, 54962, 345
  USA, New York, 67013, 678
  USA, Boston, 45824, 365
  UK, London, 64002, 743
  UK, Birmingham, 44291, 572
```

```
        UK, Manchester, 40320, 534
        Germany, Berlin, 52912, 643
        Germany, Frankfurt, 61832, 678
        Germany, Munich, 35812, 325
        Japan, Tokyo, 42137, 562
        Japan, Yokohama, 55832, 753
        Japan, Osaka, 37643, 418
];
```

How to do it...

These steps show how to create a colored Treemap with `colormix`:

1. Create a new block chart. Add **Country**, then **City** as dimensions.

2. Add the following expression:

    `Sum(Sales)`

3. Click on **Finish**:

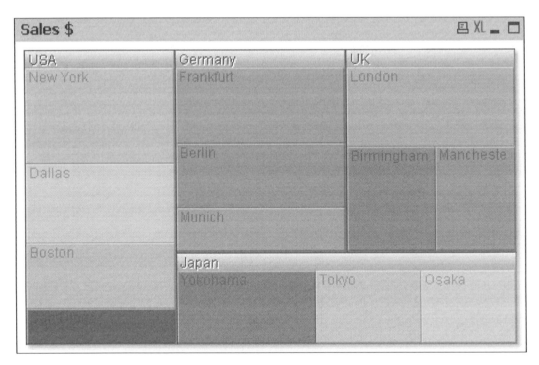

4. The block chart will be created and will display the **Sales $** values in the hierarchical sized blocks. Edit the properties of the chart to set the color.

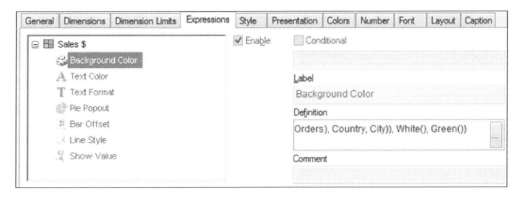

5. Click on **+** beside the **Sales $** expression, and enter the following **Background Color** expression in the **Definition** box:

```
ColorMix1(
  (Sum(Sales)/Sum(Orders))/
  Max(Total Aggr(Sum(Sales)/Sum(Orders), Country, City)),
  White(),
  Green()
)
```

6. Click on **OK**.

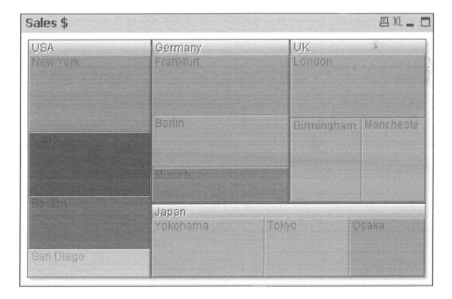

How it works...

The trick here lies in the AGGR expression:

```
(Sum(Sales)/Sum(Orders))/
Max(Total Aggr(Sum(Sales)/Sum(Orders), Country, City))
```

The Max AGGR part will return the highest value of the average sale for all of the cities. By dividing this value into the average sale for the current city, we will get a value between 0 and 1, representing the rank of that city.

TOTAL in **Max** makes sure that the dimensions are ignored for that calculation. Otherwise the calculation would only calculate for the current city and the value would be 1 for all cities:

Country	City	Sum (Sales)/Sum (Orders)	(Sum (Sales)/Sum (Orders))/ Max(Total Ag...
Germany	Berlin	82.289	0.517
Germany	Frankfurt	91.198	0.572
Germany	Munich	110.191	0.692
Japan	Osaka	90.055	0.565
Japan	Tokyo	74.977	0.471
Japan	Yokohama	74.146	0.465
UK	Birmingham	77.432	0.486
UK	London	86.140	0.541
UK	Manchester	75.506	0.474
USA	Boston	125.545	0.788
USA	Dallas	159.310	1.000
USA	New York	98.839	0.620
USA	San Diego	44.995	0.282

In this case, **Dallas** has the highest average sales, so will be **1.000**. **San Diego** has the lowest average sales at **0.282**.

When we plug those values into the ColorMix1 expression, it returns a color that is along a scale from 0 to 1 of the start and end color.

The upshot is that **Dallas** has a dark green color while San Diego has a much lighter color; closer to white.

There's more...

This use of AGGR to calculate a value across dimensions like this is very typical. It is quite a common use case.

Using RangeSum to calculate a rolling total in a multidimension table

In a single dimensional chart, for example, bar chart, line chart, or straight table, the usual way to create a rolling total is to use the `accumulate` option in the expression. This doesn't work correctly in a multi-dimensional situation.

In this recipe, we will look at creating accumulations by using the `RangeSum` function.

Getting ready

Load the following script:

```
LOAD * INLINE [
  Country, City, Sales, Orders
  USA, San Diego, 24567, 546
  USA, Dallas, 54962, 345
  USA, New York, 67013, 678
  USA, Boston, 45824, 365
  UK, London, 64002, 743
  UK, Birmingham, 44291, 572
  UK, Manchester, 40320, 534
  Germany, Berlin, 52912, 643
  Germany, Frankfurt, 61832, 678
  Germany, Munich, 35812, 325
  Japan, Tokyo, 42137, 562
  Japan, Yokohama, 55832, 753
  Japan, Osaka, 37643, 418
];
```

How to do it...

Use these steps to calculate the rolling totals with `RangeSum`:

1. Create a new pivot table with **Year** and **Country** as dimensions.

2. Add the following three expressions:

Sales $	Sum(Sales)
Country Total	RangeSum(Above(Sum(Sales), 0, RowNo()))
Overall Total	RangeSum(Above(TOTAL Sum(Sales), 0, RowNo(TOTAL)))

3. Click on **Finish** to save the chart.

Year	Country	Sales $	Country Total	Overall Total
	⊟ Japan	2765	2765	2765
2010	UK	4512	7277	7277
	USA	6013	13290	13290
	⊟ Japan	2567	2567	15857
2011	UK	3976	6543	19833
	USA	5295	11838	25128
	⊟ Japan	3111	3111	28239
2012	UK	4691	7802	32930
	USA	5551	13353	38481
	⊟ Japan	3234	3234	41715
2013	UK	5276	8510	46991
	USA	6932	15442	53923

4. Expand the **Year** dimension so that you can see all the values. Notice the rolling totals.

How it works...

The Above function allows us to specify which row "above" the current row to return and the number of rows to return. By specifying 0 for the row to start on, we are telling above to start at the current row. We then use one of the RowNo() functions to define how many rows to return.

RowNo() by itself will return the number of the rows you are on for each of the second dimension values within the first dimension (rows of **Country** within each **Year**). This resets as the first dimension value changes.

RowNo(TOTAL) will ignore the dimensions and just give us the number of the row that we are on in the whole chart.

The preceding statement will return a range of values. That is why we need to use the RangeSum function to add up all of the values returned.

There's more...

Similar to `Above`, there is a function called `Below`. There are also functions called `Before` and `After`, which you can use in a pivot table, where one of the dimensions is pivoted across the top of the chart to give us horizontal totals.

Showing only the top 3 values in a pivot table

In version 11, QlikView introduced the feature **Dimension Limits** for most of the charts. This feature allows you to limit the number of values displayed based on a certain criteria; most usually, the value is in the top X (whatever X you want). It also allows you to include an **Others** dimension value for everything else outside the top X.

This feature is not available for gauge charts (which don't usually have a dimension anyway) and pivot tables.

In this recipe, we are going to implement the feature using `AGGR` in a pivot table.

Getting ready

Load the following script:

```
LOAD * INLINE [
  Year, Country, Sales
  2010, USA, 6013
  2011, USA, 5295
  2012, USA, 5551
  2013, USA, 6932
  2010, UK, 4512
  2011, UK, 3976
  2012, UK, 4691
  2013, UK, 5276
  2010, Japan, 2765
  2011, Japan, 2567
  2012, Japan, 3111
  2013, Japan, 3234
  2010, Germany, 4374
  2011, Germany, 5673
  2012, Germany, 4322
  2013, Germany, 7654
```

```
        2010, France,    4965
        2011, France,    5097
        2012, France,    5419
        2013, France,    5732
        2010, Australia, 3966
        2011, Australia, 4087
        2012, Australia, 2376
        2013, Australia, 3784
    ];
```

How to do it...

These steps show you how to show only the top 3 values in a pivot table:

1. Create a new pivot table with **Country** and **Year** as dimensions.

2. Add the following expression for **Sales $**:

   `Sum(Sales)`

3. Click on **Finish** to save the chart.

Yearly Sales by Country

Country	Year	2010	2011	2012	2013	Total
Australia		3966	4087	2376	3784	14213
France		4965	5097	5419	5732	21213
Germany		4374	5673	4322	7654	22023
Japan		2765	2567	3111	3234	11677
UK		4512	3976	4691	5276	18455
USA		6013	5295	5551	6932	23791
Total		**26595**	**26695**	**25470**	**32612**	**111372**

4. Expand all the **Country** values and pivot the **Year** dimension across the top:

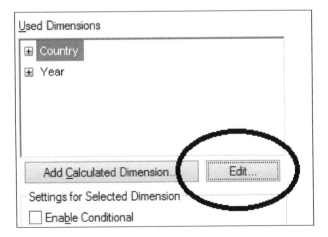

5. Edit the chart properties. On the **Dimensions** tab, select the **Country** dimension under **Used Dimensions**, and click on the **Edit** button. Enter the following expression:

```
=If(Aggr(Rank(Sum(Sales)), Country)<=3, Country, 'Others')
```

6. Edit the dimension **Label** and set it to **Country**. Click on **OK**.

Country	Year	2010	2011	2012	2013	Total
France		4965	5097	5419	5732	21213
Germany		4374	5673	4322	7654	22023
Others		11243	10630	10178	12294	44345
USA		6013	5295	5551	6932	23791
Total		**26595**	**26695**	**25470**	**32612**	**111372**

7. Note that there are now only four dimension values.

8. Edit the dimension property again and change the dimension expression to the following:

```
=If(Aggr(Rank(Sum(Sales)), Country)<=3, Country, Null())
```

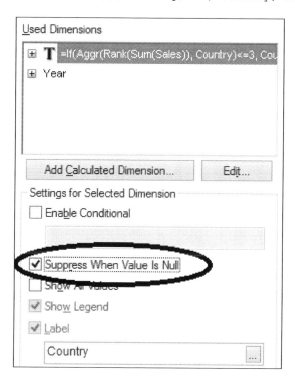

9. Turn on the option **Suppress When Value is Null**.

Yearly Sales by Country						昌 XI _ ▢
Country	Year	2010	2011	2012	2013	**Total**
France		4965	5097	5419	5732	21213
Germany		4374	5673	4322	7654	22023
USA		6013	5295	5551	6932	23791
Total		**15352**	**16065**	**15292**	**20318**	**67027**

10. Note that only the top 3 are displayed.

How it works...

Using AGGR for a calculated dimension is quite a powerful use of QlikView. In this case, we use AGGR to create an in-memory table chart of the rank of the sales for each country. We then compare the result to see if it is <= 3. If it is, the if statement returns the country, otherwise it returns something else—either Others or Null().

There's more...

It's not just using the values in an if statement that we can do; we can also use those values as the dimension in the charts. Since they are linked to the original dimension in AGGR, selecting one of these values will also select the underlying country or countries.

Creating a Statistical Control Chart using Standard Deviation

Control charts were developed by a statistician named Walter Shewhart in the 1920's. He was working for Bell Labs, who, at that time, were rolling out a telephony network across the US. For this network, amplifiers and other such equipments needed to be buried underground, and it was expensive to have to dig it up for repairs. They were worried about the variations in the manufacturing process leading to increased cost in repairs.

Shewhart used control charts to show that variation was normal and reacting to small variations by making changes to the manufacturing process was wrong. As long as the variation was within control limits and not trending in any particular direction, there was nothing to worry about.

A simple control chart uses the mean of the data (or a subset of that data) to draw a center line around which the data varies. Control limits are set at two or three standard deviations (on the basis that under a normal distribution, 95 Percent of the data should occur within two standard deviations from the mean, and 99.7 percent of the data should occur within three standard deviations).

In this recipe, we will build a control chart by using the rainfall data from London, England, to see if a recent perceived increase in rainfall was outside of the normal.

Getting ready

The rainfall data is available from the UK Met Office website. For this example, we are going to look at the data from the Heathrow weather station. The URL is `http://www.metoffice.gov.uk/climate/uk/stationdata/heathrowdata.txt`.

Let's create a new QlikView document with this data:

Load the following script:

```
LOAD @1:7 As Year,
   @8:11 As Month,
   @12:18 as [MaxTemp(C)],
   @19:26 As [MinTemp(C)],
   @27:34 as [AF Days],
   @35:42 as [Rain(mm)],
   @43:50 as [Sun Hours]
FROM
[http://www.metoffice.gov.uk/climate/uk/stationdata/heathrowdata.txt]
(fix, codepage is 1252, header is 7 lines)
Where @1:7 < 2013;
```

How to do it...

Follow these steps to create a control chart by using `Stdev`:

1. Create a new line chart with **Year** as the dimension.

2. Add the following expressions:

Rainfall(mm)	`Sum([Rain(mm)])`
Mean	`Avg({<Year=>} TOTAL Aggr(Sum({<Year=>} [Rain(mm)]), Year))`
Lower Control	`[Mean]` `-(2*Stdev({<Year=>} TOTAL Aggr(Sum({<Year=>} [Rain(mm)]), Year)))`
Upper Control	`[Mean]` `+(2*Stdev({<Year=>} TOTAL Aggr(Sum({<Year=>} [Rain(mm)]), Year)))`

Note that I have used the label of **Mean** for the second expression, and that is used as a reference in the third and fourth expressions.

3. Click on **Finish** to save the chart:

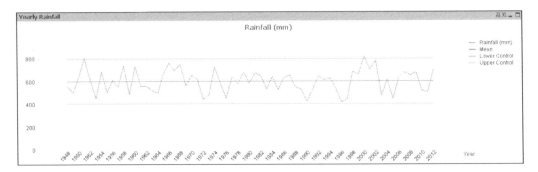

4. You should be able to see that 2012 rainfall, while being above average and above 2011 values, was within the control limits. There is no apparent trend of an increase in rainfall in the region.

How it works...

There are a couple of things going on here that are important to note. I will focus on the AVG function, as the use of the STDEV function is pretty much identical.

The AGGR functions use the TOTAL qualifier to ignore the dimensionality of the chart. This is important, otherwise the average will be the same as the yearly rainfall value; it will be an average of one value!

The second thing that is going on is that both the SUM function in the AGGR and AVG functions have a Set syntax that excludes selections on the year. This is important because we want AVG (and STDEV) to be calculated across all the data, and not to change if a user drills into a particular date (for example, by selecting in the chart).

There's more...

Standard deviation is not the only way to build a control chart. Another method to use is standard error.

Donald Wheeler, author of *Understanding Variation: The Key to Managing Chaos, SPC Press, Inc.*, suggests that there are problems with standard deviation or standard error because of the assumptions about the homogeneity of the data. Instead, he prefers a method using a moving average over an arbitrary period.

See also

▶ The *Creating a Moving Range chart* and *Creating a control chart using Moving Range* recipes in this chapter

Creating a Moving Range chart

A **Moving Range** (**mR**) chart is a way of monitoring variation to try and work out if a system is varying unexpectedly.

The range is simply calculated as the absolute difference between one data point and the previous one. We then calculate an average—usually over a specific subset of the data—of these values and apply a statistical constant (3.267 - D4 anti-biasing constant for a subgroup size of n=2). The great thing about these constants is that you don't need to understand them or how they are calculated; just that they exist.

In this recipe, we are going to use the same set of rainfall data as the previous recipe, *Creating a Statistical Control Chart using Standard Deviation*, to see how the rainfall data for Heathrow varies over time. We will use a 30-year period as our reference for what "Average" means (the UK Met office uses 1961-1990).

Getting ready

Load the data from the UK Met Office website as outlined in the previous recipe, Creating a statistical control chart using standard deviation.

How to do it...

To create a moving range chart, follow these steps:

1. Create a new line chart with **Year** as the dimension.

2. Add the following expressions:

Moving Range	`fabs(Above(Sum([Rain(mm)])))-Sum([Rain(mm)]))`
Moving Avg	`Avg({<Year={">=1961<=1990"}>} total Aggr(fabs(Above(Sum({<Year={">=1961<=1990"}>} [Rain(mm)])))-Sum({<Year={">=1961<=1990"}>} [Rain(mm)])), Year))`
Upper Control	`[Moving Avg] * 3.267`

Note that I have used the label of **Moving Avg** for the second expression and that is used as a reference in the third expression.

3. Click on **Finish** to save the chart:

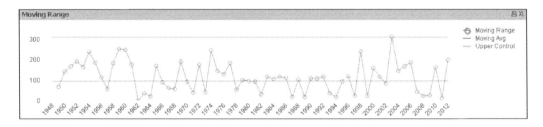

4. You should be able to see that, although the rainfall pattern varies, it generally varies within normal parameters.

How it works...

Here, we are using the ABOVE function to establish the previous value for each data point. We subtract the current data point from the previous one and use the FABS function to get the absolute (positive) value.

The Moving Avg calculation takes almost the exact same function in an AGGR statement and then obtains the average. There is one difference here, in that each aggregation function contains a Set syntax to specifically select the 1961 to 1990 year range.

There's more...

A moving average chart like this is great for visualizing the variation and seeing if the data is actually varying wildly. It provides the insight into the data that wouldn't normally be seen.

This is a great example of combining an advanced QlikView aggregation functions such as AGGR, TOTAL, and ABOVE, as well as Set Analysis.

This type of mR chart is also frequently used with a control chart, where the control limits are derived from the moving average rather than from standard deviation.

See also

▶   The *Creating a statistical control chart using standard deviation* and *Creating a control chart using Moving Range* recipes in this chapter

Creating a control chart using Moving Range

Control charts are very quickly created by using a standard deviation function for control limits. However, *Donald Wheeler*, author of *Understanding Variation: The Key to Managing Chaos, SPC Press, Inc.*, suggests that there are problems with standard deviation or standard error because of assumptions about the homogeneity of the data. Instead, he prefers a method using a moving average over an arbitrary period.

In this recipe, we are going to use the same set of rainfall data as the previous recipe, *Creating a statistical control chart using standard deviation*, to see how the rainfall data for Heathrow varies over time. Instead of using standard deviation of the data to derive the control limits, we will use the moving average (mR) and a statistical constant (2.66 – this value is obtained by dividing 3 by the sample size-specific d2 anti-biasing constant for a subgroup size of n=2).

We will use a 30-year period as our reference for what "Average" means (the UK Met office use 1961-1990).

Getting ready

Load the data from the UK Met Office website as outlined in the previous recipe, *Creating a statistical control chart using standard deviation*.

How to do it...

These steps are used to create a control chart using moving range:

1. Create a new line chart with **Year** as the dimension.
2. Add the following expressions:

Rainfall(mm)	`Sum([Rain(mm)])`
Avg	`Avg({<Year={">=1960<=1980"}>} total Aggr(Sum({<Year={">=1960<=1980"}>} [Rain(mm)]), Year))`
Upper Natural Process Limit	`[Avg] + (Avg({<Year={">=1960<=1980"}>} total Aggr(fabs(Above(Sum({<Year={">=1960<=1980"}>} [Rain(mm)]))-Sum({<Year={">=1960<=1980"}>} [Rain(mm)]))), Year)) * 2.66)`
Lower Natural Process Limit	`[Avg] - (Avg({<Year={">=1960<=1980"}>} total Aggr(fabs(Above(Sum({<Year={">=1960<=1980"}>} [Rain(mm)]))-Sum({<Year={">=1960<=1980"}>} [Rain(mm)]))), Year)) * 2.66)`

Note that I have used the label of **Avg** for the second expression, and that is used as a reference in the third and fourth expressions.

3. Click on **Finish** to save the chart:

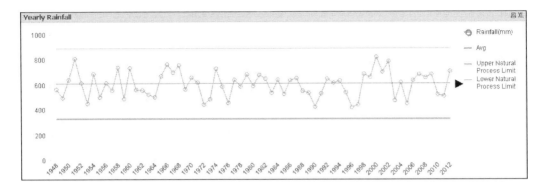

4. You should be able to see that, although the rainfall pattern varies, it is well within control limits.

How it works...

The average calculation here is a standard AGGR function, but we are using the Set syntax to specify the range of data to use as being years 1961 to 1990.

The control limits calculations use an ABOVE and FABS function to calculate the absolute difference between the values. AGGR allows us to calculate the average of this value and we then multiply by our constant.

There's more...

This type of control chart is often combined with a mR chart, and that is often called and **XmR Chart**. It is the ultimate visualization of variation and it's highly recommended to track values, especially over time.

This is a great example of combining advanced QlikView aggregation functions such as AGGR, TOTAL, and ABOVE, as well as Set Analysis.

See also

▶ The *Creating a statistical control chart using standard deviation* and *Creating a Moving Range chart* recipes in this chapter

5
Advanced Coding

In this chapter, we will cover:

- ▶ Extracting QlikView data to a Word report
- ▶ Printing reports to PDF using PDFCreator
- ▶ Creating a chart using a macro
- ▶ Using VBS functions in charts

Introduction

QlikView has a lot of great functions that enable us to manipulate data, make selections, interact with the layout, or export data to a file. These functions can be accessed from the **Actions** option of buttons, gauge charts, text objects, or line/arrow objects.

However, QlikView also has a rich API that allows us to use a macro language—either VBScript or JavaScript—to perform actions. In this chapter, we are going to explore using macros to perform some advanced tasks that are not available otherwise. We will also look at using VBScript to create functions that can be used in charts.

Documentation on the QlikView API is installed by default into `C:\ProgramData\ QlikTech\QlikView Documentation\Automation\QlikView Automation Reference.pdf`. There is also a very useful `APIGuide.qvw` file in the same folder that allows you to search the API and view sample code.

Extracting QlikView data to a Word report

While there is a good report engine in QlikView, its output is limited to printing—either to an actual printer or to a PDF printer driver. If you want to get data into a different format, for example, Word, you can manually copy and paste charts and data, but it would be useful to have a different option.

In this recipe we will use the QlikView API to extract data and use the Word API to generate that data in a Word report.

Getting ready

Load the following script:

```
LOAD * INLINE [
    Country, Sales
    UK, 100000
    USA, 101899
    Japan, 87088
    Germany, 67896
];
```

How to do it...

The following steps explain how to extract QlikView data to a Word report:

1. Create a new bar chart with `Country` as dimension. Add the following expression:

   `Sum(Sales)`

2. After clicking on **Finish** to save the chart, edit the properties and set the **Object ID** to `rptChart01`.

3. From the **Tools** menu, select **Edit Module...**.

4. Enter the following code:

   ```
   Option Explicit

   Sub SendReportToWord()
   ```

```
' Word Table formats
Const wdTableFormat3DEffects1 = 32
Const wdTableFormat3DEffects2 = 33
Const wdTableFormat3DEffects3 = 34
Const wdTableFormatClassic1 = 4
Const wdTableFormatClassic2 = 5
Const wdTableFormatClassic3 = 6
Const wdTableFormatClassic4 = 7
Const wdTableFormatColorful1 = 8
Const wdTableFormatColorful2 = 9
Const wdTableFormatColorful3 = 10
Const wdTableFormatColumns1 = 11
Const wdTableFormatColumns2 = 12
Const wdTableFormatColumns3 = 13
Const wdTableFormatColumns4 = 14
Const wdTableFormatColumns5 = 15
Const wdTableFormatContemporary = 35
Const wdTableFormatElegant = 36
Const wdTableFormatGrid1 = 16
Const wdTableFormatGrid2 = 17
Const wdTableFormatGrid3 = 18
Const wdTableFormatGrid4 = 19
Const wdTableFormatGrid5 = 20
Const wdTableFormatGrid6 = 21
Const wdTableFormatGrid7 = 22
Const wdTableFormatGrid8 = 23
Const wdTableFormatList1 = 24
Const wdTableFormatList2 = 25
Const wdTableFormatList3 = 26
Const wdTableFormatList4 = 27
Const wdTableFormatList5 = 28
Const wdTableFormatList6 = 29
Const wdTableFormatList7 = 30
Const wdTableFormatList8 = 31
Const wdTableFormatNone = 0
Const wdTableFormatProfessional = 37
Const wdTableFormatSimple1 = 1
Const wdTableFormatSimple2 = 2
Const wdTableFormatSimple3 = 3
Const wdTableFormatSubtle1 = 38
Const wdTableFormatSubtle2 = 39
Const wdTableFormatWeb1 = 40
```

```
        Const wdTableFormatWeb2 = 41
        Const wdTableFormatWeb3 = 42

        ' Create a Word object
        Dim objWord
        Set objWord = CreateObject("Word.Application")

        If Not IsObject(objWord) Then
         MsgBox "Microsoft Word cannot be found."
         Exit Sub
        End If

Dim objDoc
Dim oRange
    Set objDoc = objWord.Documents.Add
    Set oRange = objDoc.Range

    InsertHeaderToWord oRange, "QlikView Report"

    InsertTableToWord oRange, "rptChart01", _
        wdTableFormatClassic1, False
      ' Set the last parameter to True
      ' to Bold the last row (e.g. Totals)

    InsertChartToWord oRange, "rptChart01"

    InsertFooterToWord oRange

    'Finish the Document & Show it.
    objWord.Visible = True
    ' Clean up the object
    Set objWord = Nothing

End Sub

Sub InsertHeaderToWord(byref oRange, vHeaderText)

    ' Add a header
    oRange.SetRange oRange.End, oRange.End
    oRange.InsertAfter vHeaderText
    oRange.Style = "Heading 1"
    oRange.InsertParagraphAfter
```

```
      oRange.SetRange oRange.End, oRange.End
      oRange.Style = "Normal"
      oRange.InsertParagraphAfter
      oRange.SetRange oRange.End, oRange.End

End Sub

Sub InsertFooterToWord(byref oRange)

   oRange.SetRange oRange.End, oRange.End
   oRange.InsertAfter "_____"
   oRange.SetRange oRange.End, oRange.End
   oRange.InsertParagraphAfter

End Sub

Sub InsertTableToWord(byref oRange, _
     vChart, _
     vTableFormat, _
     vLastRow)

     Const wdAutoFitWindow = 2
     Const wdAutoFitContent = 1
     Const wdWord9TableBehavior = 1
     Const wdSeparateByTabs = 1

   ' Insert the table of data and format it
   Dim oTable
   oRange.InsertAfter _
   ActiveDocument.GetSheetObject(vChart).GetTableAsText(true)
   Set oTable = _
       oRange.ConvertToTable(wdSeparateByTabs, , , , _
          vTableFormat, True, True, True, True, True, _
        vLastRow, False, False, True, _
         wdAutoFitWindow, wdWord9TableBehavior)

   oTable.AutoFitBehavior (wdAutoFitWindow)

   oRange.SetRange oRange.End, oRange.End
   oRange.InsertParagraphAfter
   oRange.SetRange oRange.End, oRange.End
```

```
        End Sub


        Sub InsertChartToWord(byref oRange, vChart)

          Const wdAlignParagraphCenter = 1
          Const wdAlignParagraphLeft = 0

          ' Insert the image
          Dim vPath
          vPath = ExportBMPToFile(vChart)

          if vPath <> "" Then

            Dim oShape
            Set oShape=oRange.InlineShapes.AddPicture(vPath, _
              False, True)

            oRange.ParagraphFormat.Alignment = _
                wdAlignParagraphCenter

            ' Insert a new line after the chart
            oRange.SetRange oShape.Range.End, oShape.Range.End
            oRange.InsertParagraphAfter
            oRange.SetRange oRange.End, oRange.End
            oRange.InsertParagraphAfter
            oRange.ParagraphFormat.Alignment = _
                wdAlignParagraphLeft
            oRange.SetRange oRange.End, oRange.End

          Else
            oRange.ParagraphFormat.Alignment = _
              wdAlignParagraphCenter
            oRange.InsertAfter "Failed to insert chart " & _
              vChart
            oRange.InsertParagraphAfter
            oRange.SetRange oRange.End, oRange.End
            oRange.ParagraphFormat.Alignment = _
              wdAlignParagraphLeft
            oRange.SetRange oRange.End, oRange.End
          End if

        End Sub
```

```
Function ExportBMPToFile(vChart)

  Dim rVal, obj, vTempFileName
  rVal = ""

  vTempFileName = GetTempBMPFileName()

  ' Necessary because the WaitForIdle can throw errors
  On Error Resume Next
  Err.Clear

  set obj = ActiveDocument.GetSheetObject(vChart)

  obj.GetSheet().Activate
  obj.Activate
  ActiveDocument.GetApplication.WaitForIdle 1000

  Err.Clear

  Dim vResult
  vResult = obj.ExportEx (vTempFileName, 2)

  if vResult then rVal = vTempFileName

  On Error Goto 0

  ExportBMPToFile = rVal

End Function

Function GetTempBMPFileName()
  ' Get the Temp Folder
  Dim FSO
  Set FSO = CreateObject("Scripting.FileSystemObject")

  Dim vFolder
  Set vFolder = FSO.GetSpecialFolder(2)

  Dim vFileName
  vFileName = fso.GetTempName() & ".bmp"

  Set FSO = Nothing
  GetTempBMPFileName = vFolder & "\" & vFileName

End Function
```

5. When you have entered all the code, click on the **Check** button to perform a syntax check on the code. If all is well, the list of subroutines and functions will appear in the list below the **Check** button.

6. Change **Requested Module Security** to **System Access** and **Current Local Security** to **Allow System Access**:

7. Click on **OK** to save the code. Save the QlikView document and close QlikView.

8. Reopen QlikView and open the document. Because the module has been flagged as **System Access**, you will need to choose **Allow any Macro (only for trusted documents)**; otherwise, the macro will not be able to generate the Word document:

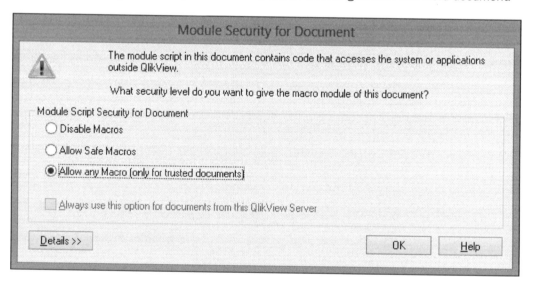

9. Add a new button to the QlikView document. Set the action of the button to **External / Run Macro**. Set **Macro Name** to SendReportToWord:

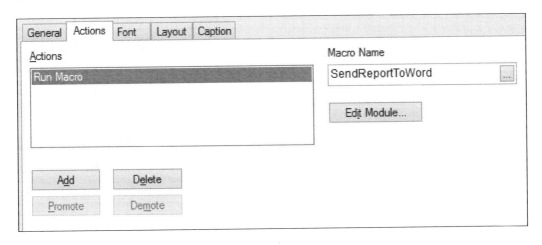

10. Click on the button and note that the report is generated in Word:

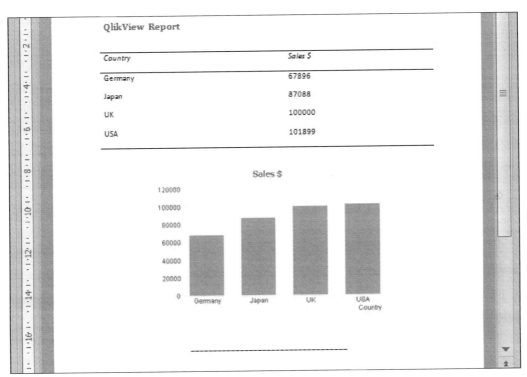

How it works...

This macro is a fairly straightforward example of the Word automation. There are two main methods, `InsertChartToWord` and `InsertTableToWord`.

`InsertTableToWord` calls the QlikView chart API method, `GetTableAsText`. This method returns the data behind the chart in a tab delimited format. We then format this using a Word function.

`InsertChartToWord` first uses the QlikView chart API method, `ExportEx`. This exports the image of the chart to a bitmap file, which we can then import into the Word document.

There's more...

This exports data to Word, but of course, you can use similar techniques to export data and charts to any other application that supports similar API calls, such as Excel or PowerPoint.

See also

> ▶ The *Printing reports to PDF using PDFCreator* recipe

Printing reports to PDF using PDFCreator

QlikView's report engine is very capable of producing good quality paper or PDF reports (with an appropriate PDF printer driver). There is an additionally licensed add-on for QlikView Publisher that allows automated generation of these reports into PDF and distribution to multiple recipients. This additional option is not available without Publisher.

This recipe demonstrates using automation to print the reports using the PDFCreator (http://sourceforge.net/projects/pdfcreator) printer driver. This driver has its own API that allows us to control the name of the file and location.

 Note that when installing PDFCreator, you should watch out for additional toolbars or add-ons that you may not want to install.

The code has been tested on versions of PDFCreator up to 1.6.2, but I would expect it to work on newer versions.

Getting ready

This example can use any QlikView document that has a report. I am going to assume that there is at least one report called RP01—change the report ID to match your own document. I am also assuming that there is a field called Country, for which I am going to create a PDF for each value in that field. Again, change this to match your document.

How to do it...

Use the following steps to print QlikView reports to PDF using PDFCreator:

1. From the **Tools** menu, select **Edit Module...**.
2. Enter the following code:

```
Option Explicit

Sub PrintReport()

    ActiveDocument.ClearAll

    Dim FieldName

    FieldName = "Country"

    Dim mySelections

    set mySelections = _
       ActiveDocument.Fields(FieldName).GetPossibleValues

    Dim i

    for i = 0 to mySelections.Count - 1

        Dim FieldValue

        FieldValue = mySelections.Item(i).text

        ActiveDocument.Fields(FieldName).Select FieldValue

        Print_PDF FieldValue, "My Report", "RP01"

    Next

End Sub
```

```
Sub Print_PDF(FieldValue, ReportName, ReportID)

  ' This is mostly reference code from the
  ' PDF Creator documentation

    ' Designed for early bind, set reference to PDFCreator
    Dim pdfjob
    Dim sPDFName
    Dim sPDFPath

    '/// Change the output file name here! ///
    sPDFName = ReportName & " - " & FieldValue
    sPDFPath = "C:\Temp"

    Set pdfjob = CreateObject("PDFCreator.clsPDFCreator")

    With pdfjob

      If .cStart("/NoProcessingAtStartup") = False Then
        If .cStart("/NoProcessingAtStartup", True) = _
        False Then

          Exit Sub
        End if
        .cVisible = True
      End If

      .cOption("UseAutosave") = 1
      .cOption("UseAutosaveDirectory") = 1
      .cOption("AutosaveDirectory") = sPDFPath
      .cOption("AutosaveFilename") = sPDFName
      .cOption("AutosaveFormat") = 0 ' 0 = PDF
      .cClearCache

    End With

    ' Print the QlikView Report
    ActiveDocument.PrintReport ReportID, "PDFCreator"

    ' Wait until the print job has entered the print queue
    Do Until pdfjob.cCountOfPrintjobs = 1
     ActiveDocument.GetApplication.Sleep 20
        ' in VBScript use WScript.Sleep(20)
    Loop
    pdfjob.cPrinterStop = False

    ' Wait until PDF creator is finished
```

```
' then release the objects
Do Until pdfjob.cCountOfPrintjobs = 0
 ActiveDocument.GetApplication.Sleep 20
Loop
pdfjob.cClose
Set pdfjob = Nothing

End Sub
```

3. Click on **OK** to save the code. Save the QlikView document and close QlikView.

4. Reopen QlikView and open the document. Because the module has been flagged as **System Access**, you will need to choose **Allow any Macro (only for trusted documents)**; otherwise, the macro will not be able to generate the PDF document.

5. Add a new button to the QlikView document. Set the action of the button to **External / Run Macro**. Set **Macro Name** to `PrintReport`:

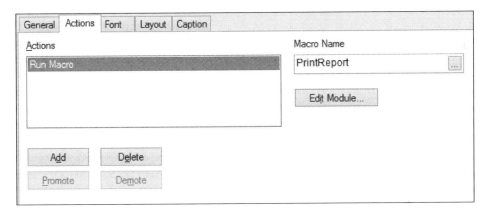

6. Click on the button and confirm that the PDFs are created for each country (or other field that you have chosen) in the selected folder.

How it works...

This is a good example of using the QlikView API to select different values in a field.

The `GetPossibleValues` method of the QlikView fields object will return an array of all the values in a field. We call `ClearAll` first to make sure that we have access to all the values. This is, of course, optional and you can run it with current selections instead.

We then loop through all the values and call the **Select** method to select each value in turn and then call the `Print` method of the document to print to PDF.

▸ The *Extracting QlikView data to a Word report* recipe

Creating a chart using a macro

This is quite an advanced topic and not something that you will need to do very often. But it is a great thing to have in your arsenal – being able to generate a chart based on user entry is a useful thing to be able to do.

Getting ready

Load the following script:

```
LOAD * INLINE [
   Country, Sales
   UK, 100000
   USA, 101899
   Japan, 87088
   Germany, 67896
];
```

How to do it...

These steps show you how to create a chart using a macro:

1. From the **Tools** menu, select **Edit Module...**.
2. Enter the following code:

```
Option Explicit

Sub GenerateBarChart()

  Dim myChart

  ' Create a new Bar Chart
  Set myChart = _
     ActiveDocument.ActiveSheet().CreateBarChart()

  ' Add a dimension of Country to the new chart
  myChart.AddDimension "Country"
```

```
' Add an expression
myChart.AddExpression "Sum(Sales) "

' Get the properties object
Dim cp
Set cp = myChart.GetProperties()

' Set the title of the dimension
cp.Dimensions(0).Title.v = "Country Name"

' Set the Title-in-chart text
cp.ChartProperties.Title.Title.v = "Sales by Country"

' Set the Window title
cp.GraphLayout.WindowTitle.v = "Sales $ by Country"

' Set sort by Y-Value
cp.SortByYValue = -1

' Get the expression properties
Dim expr, exprvis
Set expr = _
 cp.Expressions.Item(0).Item(0).Data.ExpressionData
Set exprvis = _
 cp.Expressions.Item(0).Item(0).Data.ExpressionVisual

' Set the Expression label
exprvis.Label.v = "Sales $"

' Set the "Values on Data Point" option
exprvis.NumbersOnBars = -1

' Set the number format for the expression
exprvis.NumberPresentation.Dec = "."
exprvis.NumberPresentation.Fmt = "#,##0.00"
exprvis.NumberPresentation.nDec = 2
exprvis.NumberPresentation.Thou = ","
exprvis.NumberPresentation.Type = 11 'fixed
exprvis.NumberPresentation.UseThou = 1

' Apply the modified properties
myChart.SetProperties cp

End Sub
```

3. Click on **OK** to save the code. Save the QlikView document and close QlikView.

4. Add a new button to the QlikView document. Set the action of the button to **External / Run Macro**. Set **Macro Name** to GenerateBarChart:

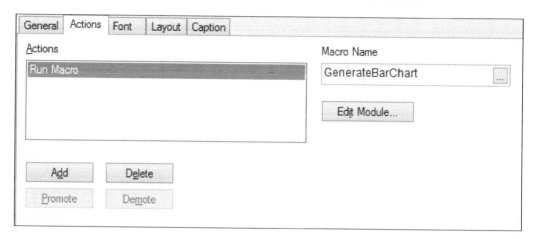

5. Click on the button and note that a new bar chart is generated.

How it works...

This uses the QlikView API to call the CreateBarChart method that generates a new chart. Once created, we then modify the properties to get the result that we were looking for.

There's more...

As well as bar charts, we can create all of the other chart types. The properties for all of the bitmap charts are pretty much the same. However, there are a few minor differences for the table charts.

There are some functions available through the API that are not present through the UI. For example, setting specific column widths.

As an even more advanced use, it is possible to allow a user to enter a query as a variable and then have this reloaded. We can use a step such as this to automatically create an appropriate chart to go with it.

Using VBS functions in charts

999 times out of 1000, we can do everything that we need to do using the embedded QlikView functions. There is just that one in a thousand awkward times, where there is a calculation that is just not calculable by combining those functions.

In this recipe we will examine the `Days360` function. This function calculates the number of days between two dates based on a 360 day year, that is, 30 days per whole month. There is a slightly different calculation between Europe and the U.S., so we will take that into account.

Getting ready

We don't need a special QlikView document here. Any document will do.

How to do it...

These steps show you how to use a VBS function in a chart:

1. From the **Tools** menu, select **Edit Module...**.
2. Enter the following code:

```
Option Explicit

Function Days360(StartDate, EndDate, European)

  Dim Days1, Days2
  Days1 = Day(EndDate)
  Days2 = Day(StartDate)

  If European and Days1 = 31 Then Days1 = 30
  If European and Days2 = 31 Then Days2 = 30

  Days360 = _
  DATEDIFF("m", StartDate, EndDate) * 30 + Days1 - Days2

End Function
```

3. Click on **OK** to save the code.
4. From the **Help** menu, select **About**.

5. Right-click on the QlikView ball in the lower, left-hand corner. In the **Settings** menu that appears, locate and select the **AllowMacroFunctionInExpressions** option. Enter the value of 1 and click on **Set**:

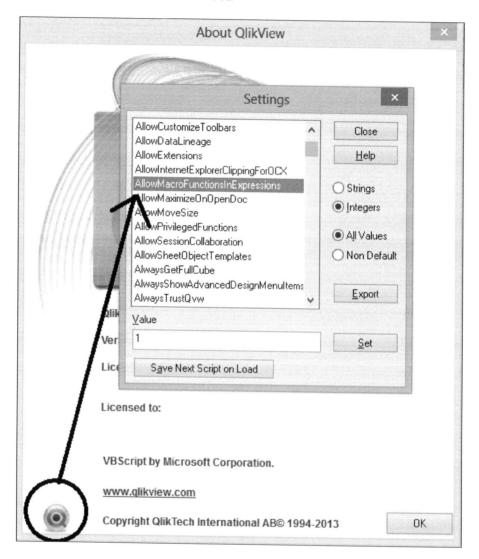

6. Close the **Settings** dialog and the **About** dialog.

7. Save the QlikView document and close QlikView. It is necessary to close and re-open QlikView to have this new setting apply.

8. Re-open QlikView and either open a new document or add a new document.

9. Add a text object and enter the following expression:

```
=Days360('1/1/2010','31/12/2011',-1)
```

Note that the value of **719** should be displayed. If you change the third parameter from -1 (true) to 0 (false), the value should be **720**.

How it works...

By turning the **AllowMacroFunctionInExpressions** option on, we enable QlikView objects to access VBScript functions.

It is important to note that the VBScript engine is single threaded, so these functions will perform less well than any native QlikView function.

It is also important to note that these types of options are not necessarily fully supported by QlikTech.

There's more...

Functions in the module can also be called from the load script! This could be a useful addition to your solution.

6
Data Modeling

In this chapter, we will cover:

- ▸ Concatenation of fact tables to avoid loops and synthetic keys
- ▸ Creating a Key/Link table in QlikView

Introduction

Data modeling in QlikView is usually quite straightforward. Often we will need to rename some fields to prevent associations that shouldn't be there, or rename a field to make an association.

Sometimes we are faced with a situation where things are not quite easy. There may be multiple fact tables with multiple associations to other tables that cause the "dreaded" synthetic key or, worse, a data loop.

A good data model in QlikView is often very different from one that might be built for an operational database. Often the best design approach is quite akin to dimensional modeling. Depending on the complexity of the data, a hybrid of approaches is necessary and QlikView is flexible enough to support this.

In this chapter, we will examine strategies to deal with these more complex associations.

Concatenation of fact tables to avoid loops and synthetic keys

Probably, the most common situation that requires more complex data modeling is where we have more than one fact table—a table containing a number that we might use in a calculation—all of which have several common key fields linking to other dimension tables.

There are several ways to deal with this situation; by far the easiest way is to simply concatenate the fact tables together to form one large fact table. The result is often a typical star or snowflake schema.

Getting ready

Load the following script:

```
Store:
Load * Inline [
StoreID, StoreName
1, Store A
2, Store B
];

Calendar:
Load MonthID As DateID, Month Inline [
MonthID, Month
1, Jan
2, Feb
];

Product:
Load * Inline [
ProductID, Product
1, Product A
2, Product B
];

Sales:
LOAD * INLINE [
    DateID, StoreID, ProductID, SaleQty, SaleValue
    1, 1, 1, 2, 23
    1, 1, 2, 4, 24
```

```
        2, 1, 1, 4, 33
        2, 1, 2, 3, 28
        1, 2, 1, 2, 21
        1, 2, 2, 4, 30
        2, 2, 1, 3, 25
];

Waste:
LOAD * INLINE [
        DateID, StoreID, ProductID, WasteQty, WasteValue
        1, 1, 1, 1, 10
        2, 1, 2, 1, 9
        1, 2, 2, 2, 17
        2, 2, 2, 1, 8
];
```

Note that the data schema contains a synthetic key.

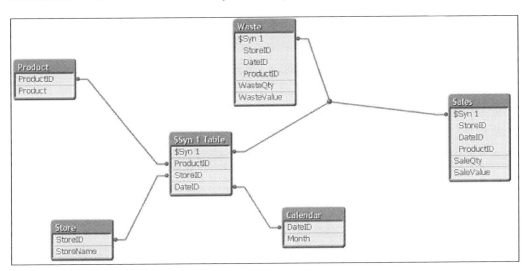

How to do it...

1. Edit the script and modify the Waste table load as follows:

    ```
    //Waste:
    Concatenate (Sales)
    LOAD * INLINE [
        DateID, StoreID, ProductID, WasteQty, WasteValue
    ```

```
        1,  1,  1,  1,  10
        2,  1,  2,  1,  9
        1,  2,  2,  2,  17
        2,  2,  2,  1,  8
    ];
```

2. Reload the script.

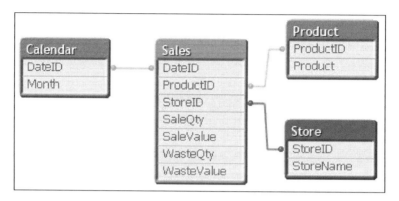

Note that the synthetic key has been removed.

StoreID	DateID	ProductID	SaleQty	SaleValue	WasteQty	WasteValue
2	1	1	2	21	-	-
1	1	1	2	23	-	-
1	1	1	-	-	1	10
1	1	2	4	24	-	-
2	1	2	4	30	-	-
2	1	2	-	-	2	17
2	2	1	3	25	-	-
1	2	1	4	33	-	-
1	2	2	3	28	-	-
1	2	2	-	-	1	9
2	2	2	-	-	1	8

Note that the Sales table contains data for both sales and waste quantities and values, but they are on different lines.

How it works...

This works very well because of the way QlikView associations work and the fact that QlikView ignores null values for the purposes of calculations. So, even though we have nulls on several rows, these will just be ignored and the expressions will calculate correctly for the associated keys.

If I select a particular store, the sum of `SalesValue` for the store will still be calculated correctly as will the sum of `WasteValue`, and both of those expressions can be juxtaposed in a chart.

It is worth noting that you can achieve rows of data with different granularity (for example, rows of sales with product and store but rows of budget that only have product and no store) with this method, and you should think carefully about what happens in this case. It is possible to use set expressions to allow different values to calculate under different selections, but it is not always valid to do so.

There's more...

Another approach might be to try and join the two tables using the common key values. This would only work if each combination of keys was unique in both tables (which it might be if you are using preaggregated data). If it isn't, you would end up with Cartesian joins of and duplicate, triplicate, etc. values. If there were missing values in either table, that would also cause issues.

One way to watch out for this is to count the number of rows in each table and count the number of rows in the resulting table. If there is a significant increase in rows, you might have a Cartesian issue.

See also

  ▸ The *Creating a Key/Link table in QlikView* recipe

Creating a Key/Link table in QlikView

Where there are fact tables that mostly share a set of keys, concatenation should always be considered first. However, where there are many more keys in one fact table than another, and the additional keys are not relevant to the second table, it may be a better approach to create a key table to link the common keys.

In this recipe, we are going to create a budget for store and product but not put any date on this.

Getting ready

Load the following script:

```
Store:
Load * Inline [
```

```
StoreID, StoreName
1, Store A
2, Store B
];

Calendar:
Load MonthID As DateID, Month Inline [
MonthID, Month
1, Jan
2, Feb
];

Product:
Load * Inline [
ProductID, Product
1, Product A
2, Product B
];

Sales:
LOAD * INLINE [
    DateID, StoreID, ProductID, SaleQty, SaleValue
    1, 1, 1, 2, 23
    1, 1, 2, 4, 24
    2, 1, 1, 4, 33
    2, 1, 2, 3, 28
    1, 2, 1, 2, 21
    1, 2, 2, 4, 30
    2, 2, 1, 3, 25
];

Budget:
LOAD * INLINE [
    StoreID, ProductID, BudgetQty, BudgetValue
    1, 1, 5, 50
    1, 2, 6, 47
    2, 1, 5, 41
    2, 2, 4, 27
];
```

Note that the data schema contains a synthetic key.

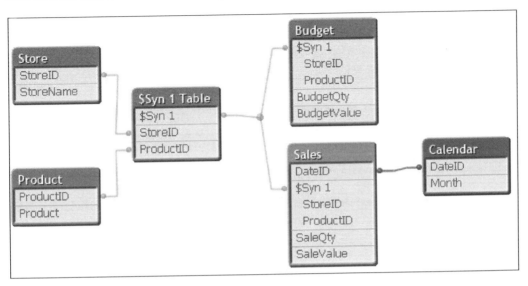

How to do it...

1. Create a key field for the `Sales` and `Budget` tables that contains the common key fields.

   ```
   Sales:
   LOAD
       AutoNumberHash256(StoreID, ProductID) As SalesBudgetID,
       *
   INLINE [
           DateID, StoreID, ProductID, SaleQty, SaleValue
           1, 1, 1, 2, 23
           1, 1, 2, 4, 24
           2, 1, 1, 4, 33
           2, 1, 2, 3, 28
           1, 2, 1, 2, 21
           1, 2, 2, 4, 30
           2, 2, 1, 3, 25
   ];
   ```

```
Budget:
LOAD
  AutoNumberHash256(StoreID, ProductID) As SalesBudgetID,
  *
INLINE [
    StoreID, ProductID, BudgetQty, BudgetValue
    1, 1, 5, 50
    1, 2, 6, 47
    2, 1, 5, 41
    2, 2, 4, 27
];
```

2. Start to build the `Key` table from the data in the `Sales` table.

```
Key:
Load Distinct
  SalesBudgetID,
  StoreID,
  ProductID
Resident
  Sales;
```

3. Join all the matching values from the `Budget` table.

```
Join (Key)
Load Distinct
  SalesBudgetID,
  StoreID,
  ProductID
Resident
  Budget;
```

4. Finally, we drop the fields in the `Sales` and `Budget` tables that are now in the `Key` table.

```
// These fields are no longer needed in the fact tables
Drop Fields StoreID, ProductID From Sales;
Drop Fields StoreID, ProductID From Budget;
```

5. Reload the script.

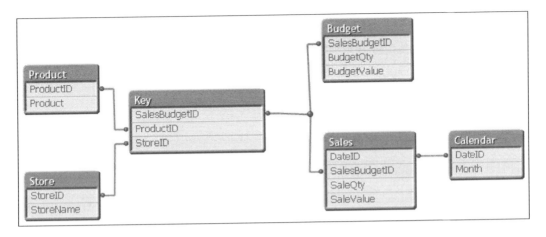

Note that the synthetic key is gone.

How it works...

The `Join` load here, which is a full outer join, combines all the possible values from both tables into the `Key` table. Any selection on the product or store will still associate correctly to the fact values. The `Distinct` clause in `Load` ensures that only unique values are added to the `Key` table.

`AutoNumberHash265` is a function that accepts a number of values and will always return the same integer if the same values are passed again. It is very useful for converting several key values into one integer key. You should note that it only works to return the same integer when used within the same load script. It would not be valid to use in different load scripts that might store the data in QVDs.

There's more...

In this case, we created the same key in both the tables. This is not always the case; as long as the key can associate correctly to the fact table, any key will do. A primary key from the fact table is often used.

See also

▶ The *Concatenation of fact tables to avoid loops and synthetic keys* recipe

7
Extensions

In this chapter, we will cover:

- ▶ Creating a simple HTML extension
- ▶ Creating a simple HTML table
- ▶ Creating an interactive extension
- ▶ Using external libraries with extensions

Introduction

QlikView has always had a great selection of chart objects to allow you to display data. There are eleven graphical chart types with various display options, and two table charts.

There has always been demand for new chart types but many of which would only be used in specific circumstances and QlikView charts have more general application. So, with Version 10, QlikView introduced a new way of displaying data—Extension Objects, which allows developers to create their own chart types to display QlikView data in whatever way they want.

An extension object allows us to create a table, chart, other data visualization, or other extension to the AJAX user interface, using HTML and JavaScript. This allows us to consume a third-party Flash or Silverlight object. We can also consume other JavaScript libraries, such as D3 or Raphaël. In fact, since Version 11 of QlikView, the commonly used jQuery library is available to developers without having to add it separately.

Our chart can use data from QlikView and we can also have it pass click events back to QlikView to make selections. With this ability, we can basically make any type of data visualization that you could imagine.

There could be a whole lot of work to do to create this, but that is really just the piece to create the actual visualization. It is actually really simple to get a chart up and running and consuming QlikView data.

It is worth noting that, because extensions are a HTML- and JavaScript-based technology, it is only available in the QlikView AJAX **Zero-Footprint Client** (**ZFC**). Extensions do not work in the QlikView plugin client. We can use them in QlikView Desktop, but only if we turn on the **WebView** mode.

For desktop users (that means all developers), the extension objects live in this folder:

```
%UserProfile%\AppData\Local\QlikTech\QlikView\Extensions\Objects
```

%UserProfile% is usually something like
C:\Users\your.username.

Each extension must have a folder for itself. However, you can have multiple subfolder levels if you want. So, you might have a subfolder under `Objects` with your company name, and then several subfolders under that, one for each extension.

When deploying to a QlikView server, the `Objects` folder defaults to:

```
%ProgramData%\QlikTech\QlikViewServer\Extensions\Objects
```

However, you can change this in the server configuration (which would be recommended for cluster deployments).

Documentation on the JavaScript API for Version 11 can be found on the QlikView Community at `http://community.qlikview.com/docs/DOC-2673`.

This chapter focusses on extension objects, but there is another type of extension that you can create in QlikView 11 called **Document Extensions**. Extension objects behave like other QlikView objects whereas Document Extensions act at the document level. Common examples of their use are to change the default behavior of the QlikView display, such as changing the tab row into a different format.

Creating a simple HTML extension

This is the simplest possible extension, but actually one that is potentially very useful. By having a dynamic URL, we can display whatever data we want in the extension—essentially an iFrame.

Getting ready

Load the following script:

```
Sales:
LOAD * INLINE [
    Country, Sales
    USA, 1000
    Mexico, 600
    Canada, 700
    UK, 900
    Germany, 800
];
```

How to do it...

Follow these steps to create a simple extension:

1. Open your user profile folder (usually `C:\Users\your.username`) and browse down to `AppData\Local\QlikTech\QlikView\Extensions\Objects`.

   You may need to create the `Extensions\Objects` folder if no extensions have been previously installed.

2. Create a new subfolder in the `Objects` folder and call it `QlikViewCookbook`. Create a subfolder in here and call it `HTMLPage`.

3. In this folder, create a text file called `Definition.xml`. Enter the following XML into this file and save it:

   ```
   <?xml version="1.0" encoding="utf-8"?>
   <ExtensionObject Label="QlikView Cookbook HTML Page">
   <Text Label="URL" Initial="" Expression="='about:blank'"/>
   </ExtensionObject>
   ```

4. Create another text file and name it `Script.js`. Enter the following code into this file and save it:

   ```
   Qva.AddExtension('QlikViewCookbook/HTMLPage', function() {
       // Set the HTML
       var _this = this;
       var frameTag = "<iframe src='"
           + _this.Layout.Text0.text
           + "' style='height: "
           + _this.GetHeight()
           + "px; width: "
   ```

```
        + _this.GetWidth()
        + "px; margin: 0; padding: 0; border: none'></iframe>"
    _this.Element.innerHTML = frameTag;
},true);
```

5. Open the QlikView document. Add a list box for the `Country` field.

6. From the **View** menu, select **Turn on/off WebView**. If you have the **Design Toolbar** enabled, the last button performs the same action.

7. Right-click on the sheet and select **New Sheet Object** from the menu:

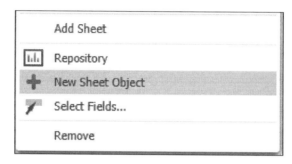

8. Click on the **Extension Objects** menu. Drag a **QlikView Cookbook HTML Page** object onto the sheet. Close the **New Sheet Object** dialog.

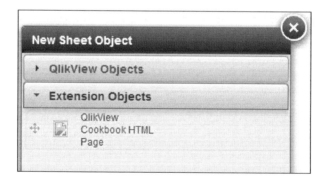

9. Right-click on the caption of the new object and select **Properties** from the menu.

 Note that if you right-click in the middle of the object that you are getting the menu for the hosted web page, not the QlikView extension object.

Enter the following expression for the URL (you can use the **fx** button to assist):

```
=if(len(Only(Country))>0,
'http://en.wikipedia.org/wiki/' & Country,
'about:blank')
```

10. Select a country in the list box. If only one is selected, the web page for that country should display.

How it works...

The `Definition` file is an XML file that describes the properties of the object. It is possible to create a file called `Properties.qvpp` that defines how these should be displayed for entry in the properties dialog. We haven't done this because if you don't create the QVPP, QlikView will use the contents of the `Definition` XML file to dynamically generate one (you will see a file called `DynProperties.qvpp` in the extension folder).

In our definition file we define a label for the object, this is what displays in the **New Sheet Object** dialog. We also define one Text object with a label of `URL`. There are two other tags in here, `Initial` and `Expression`. If just `Initial` is defined, the user will have a free textbox to enter the value. If `Expression` is defined, the **fx** button is available and the text is treated as an expression.

The rest of the magic is in the `Script.js` file. Basically, we generate an `iFrame` tag using the text from the expression. The first text object defined in the `Definition` file will be `_this.Layout.Text0.text`. The second will be `_this.Layout.Text1.text`, and so on.

Finally, we define a QlikView expression that dynamically sets the URL based on the user selection.

There's more...

Although this extension object only defines one property, all of the usual properties for other objects—caption, presentation, and so on—are available for it. This includes the show condition option. So, for example, you could have it display an order entry page, but only if the user has drilled down, perhaps, to one account.

See also

▶ The *Creating a simple HTML table* recipe

Creating a simple HTML table

We can, of course, use extension objects to pass data through to third-party controls, for example, Flash or Silverlight. But we can also fully control the way we display the data using HTML and JavaScript, especially if we employ one of the many visualization libraries available, such as D3.js.

In this example, we are going to create a simple HTML table based on the data in QlikView.

Getting ready

Load the following script:

```
Sales:
LOAD * INLINE [
    Country, Sales
    USA, 1000
    Mexico, 600
    Canada, 700
    UK, 900
    Germany, 800
];
```

How to do it...

These steps show you how to create a simple HTML table extension:

1. Open your user profile folder (usually `C:\Users\your.username`) and browse down to `AppData\Local\QlikTech\QlikView\Extensions\Objects`

   You may need to create the `Extensions\Objects` folder if no extensions have previously been installed.

2. Create a new subfolder in the `Objects` folder and call it `QlikViewCookbook`. Create a subfolder in here and call it `HTMLTable`.

3. In this folder, create a text file called `Definition.xml`. Enter the following XML into this file and save it:

   ```xml
   <?xml version="1.0" encoding="utf-8"?>
   <ExtensionObject Label="QlikView Cookbook HTML Table"
   PageHeight="10000">
   <Text Label="Dimension Label:" Initial="" Expression="Country" />
   <Dimension Label="Country:" Initial="" DropTarget="Country"/>
   ```

```
<Text Label="Expression Label:" Initial="" Expression="Sales $" />
<Measurement Label="Sales Expr:" Initial=""
Expression="Sum(Sales)" />
<Initiate Name="Caption.Text" Value="QlikView Cookbook HTML
Table"/>
<Initiate Name="Chart.BgColor.ColorHex" value="#FFF"/>
</ExtensionObject>
```

4. Create another text file and name it `Script.js`. Enter the following code into this file and save it:

```
Qva.AddExtension('QlikViewCookbook/HTMLTable', function() {
  // Load our css file
  Qva.LoadCSS("/QvAjaxZfc/QvsViewClient.aspx?public=only&name=Exte
nsions/QlikViewCookbook/HTMLTable/style.css");

  var _this = this;

  // Headings
  var DimLabel = _this.Layout.Text0.text;
  var ExprLabel = _this.Layout.Text1.text;

  // prototype for a table row
  var headstring = "<tr class='myTable'><th class='myTable'>{0}</
th><th class='myTableR'>{1}</th></tr>"
  var rowstring = "<tr><td class='myTable'>{0}</td><td
class='myTableR'>{1}</td></tr>";

  // Create a variable to hold generated html
  var html = "<table class='myTable'>";

  html += headstring.format(DimLabel, ExprLabel);

  // Cycle Through the data
  for (var i = 0; i < _this.Data.Rows.length; i++) {
    // get the row
    var row = _this.Data.Rows [i];

    // Generate html
    html += rowstring.format(row[0].text, addCommas(row[1].text));
  }

  // Finalize the html
  html += "</table>";
```

```
  // Set the HTML
  _this.Element.innerHTML = html;

},true);

String.prototype.format = function () {
  // code from stackoverflow.com
  var args = arguments;
  return this.replace(/\{(\d+)\}/g,
      function (m, n) { return args[n]; });
};

function addCommas(nStr)
{
  // function from mredkj.com
  nStr += '';
  x = nStr.split('.');
  x1 = x[0];
  x2 = x.length > 1 ? '.' + x[1] : '';
  var rgx = /(\d+)(\d{3})/;
  while (rgx.test(x1)) {
     x1 = x1.replace(rgx, '$1' + ',' + '$2');
  }
  return x1 + x2;
}
```

5. Create another text file and name it `style.css`. Enter the following code into this file and save it:

```
table.myTable
{
  font-family:Arial;
  width:100%;
  height:100%
  border-collapse:collapse;
}
th.myTable, td.myTable
{
  text-align:left;
  font-size:1em;
  border:1px solid #0080A0;
  padding:3px 7px 2px 7px;
}
th.myTableR, td.myTableR
```

```
{
  width: 100px;
  text-align:right;
  font-size:1em;
  border:1px solid #0080A0;
  padding:3px 7px 2px 7px;
}
```

6. Create a 24x24 `.png` image and save it into the `HTMLTable` folder as `icon.png`.

7. Open the QlikView document. Add a list box for the **Country** field.

8. From the **View** menu, select **Turn on/off WebView**.

9. Right-click on the sheet and select **New Sheet Object** from the menu:

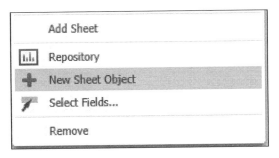

10. Click on the **Extension Objects** menu. Drag a **QlikView Cookbook HTML Table** object onto the sheet (note the icon). Close the **New Sheet Object** dialog.

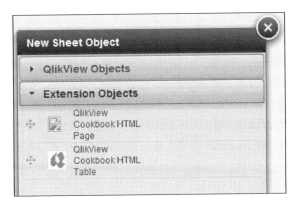

11. Right-click on the caption of the new object and select **Properties** from the menu. Note the default settings.

12. Make selections in the list box and note what happens with the extension.

How it works...

The `Definition` file defines a number of items here with default values:

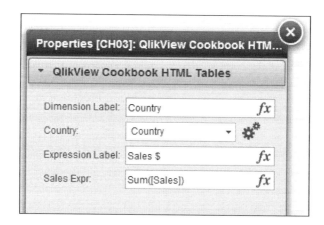

This shows how we can pass values from QlikView to the extension object.

In the `Script.js`, we access these values either as static values—as with the labels—or dynamic data from QlikView. The dimension and expression define a table of values, which you could imagine as a straight table. We can then access these values via the `Rows` property of the `Data` object.

`Rows` is an array of row objects. Each row object is also an array representing each column in the table. `row[0]` is the dimension, `row[1]` is the expression.

In the `Definition.xml` file, we have also added a `PageHeight` tag. This is in reference to the maximum number of rows that will be returned in the `Data` object per page. By default, this is `40`. You can choose to leave the page size at 40, or choose whatever size you want, and then manage the pages via the `Data.PageObject`. In this instance, I want to deal with all of the data in one go, so I set the page size to a large enough value to deliver as much data as I expect.

The other interesting thing to note here is the `Qva.LoadCSS` function that loads the external stylesheet that we have created.

There's more...

Adding additional dimensions and expressions will add additional values to the row array.

We have seen `LoadCSS` here but there is also another function called `LoadScript` that allows us to load other JavaScript files. This is how we import additional libraries such as D3 or Raphaël.

See also

▸ The *Creating a simple HTML extension* recipe

▸ The *Creating an interactive extension* recipe

▸ The *Using external libraries with extensions* recipe

Creating an interactive extension

This recipe follows on from the previous one to show how we add interactivity to our QlikView.

Getting ready

Create the extension from the *Creating a simple HTML table* recipe.

How to do it...

Follow these steps to create an interactive extension:

1. Edit the `Script.js` file. Modify the `rowstring` value like this:

```
var rowstring = "<tr><td class='myTable' onClick='onmyrowcli
ck({2});'>{0}</td><td class='myTableR'>{1}</td></tr>";
```

2. Just below this line, add this new code block:

```
// Register a function to handle the click
window.onmyrowclick = function(irow)
{
    _this.Data.SelectRow(irow);
}
```

3. Finally, modify the line that builds the HTML (under the `// Generate HTML` comment):

```
html += rowstring.format(row[0].text,
addCommas(row[1].text), i);
```

4. Save the file and open the QlikView file. Note that if you have the QlikView file open, just pressing *F5* will refresh the JavaScript.

5. Note what happens when you click a country name in the grid.

How it works...

The `SelectRow` function executes a select in the row value. Because there is only one dimension, it will make the selection of the correct country.

There's more...

Instead of `SelectRow`, you could use `SearchColumn` instead and pass the string value to look for. For example:

```
window.onmyrowclick = function(vcntry)
{
   //_this.Data.SelectRow(irow);
   _this.Data.SearchColumn(0, vcntry, false);
}
```

See also

  ▶ The *Creating a simple HTML table* recipe
  ▶ The *Using external libraries with extensions* recipe

Using external libraries with extensions

Extension objects give us great flexibility to add our own visualizations to QlikView. Even more so than when we combine them with external JavaScript libraries, which allow us to do things that just aren't possible in QlikView. Unlike using a third-party flash control, the JavaScript libraries usually give us more flexibility and control over the final output. They are usually more compatible with a wider range of clients (iPads, Android, and so on) than a control might be.

In this recipe, we are going to build a fairly simple pie chart using the Raphaël graphical library.

Getting ready

Load the following script:

```
Sales:
LOAD * INLINE [
    Country, Sales
    USA, 1000
    Mexico, 600
    Canada, 700
```

```
    UK, 900
    Germany, 800
];
```

How to do it...

These steps will show you how to use an external library with an extension:

1. Open your user profile folder (usually `c:\Users\your.username`) and browse down to `AppData\Local\QlikTech\QlikView\Extensions\Objects`.

    You may need to create the `Extensions\Objects` folder if no extensions have previously been installed.

2. Create a new subfolder in the `Objects` folder and call it `QlikViewCookbook`. Create a subfolder in here and call it `RaphaelPie`.

3. In this folder, create a text file called `Definition.xml`. Enter the following XML into this file and save it:

    ```xml
    <?xml version="1.0" encoding="utf-8"?>
    <ExtensionObject Label="QlikView Cookbook Raphael Pie">
    <Dimension Label="Country:" Initial="" DropTarget="Country"/>
    <Measurement Label="Sales Expr:" Initial=""
    Expression="Sum(Sales)" />
    <Initiate Name="Caption.Text" Value="QlikView Cookbook Raphael
    Pie"/>
    </ExtensionObject>
    ```

4. Create another text file and name it `Script.js`. Enter the following code into this file and save it:

    ```javascript
    // Load the the Raphael library
    Qva.LoadScript("http://cdnjs.cloudflare.com/ajax/libs/
    raphael/2.1.0/raphael-min.js", function() {

      // Load the Raphael graphical library
      Qva.LoadScript("http://g.raphaeljs.com/g.raphael.js", function()
    {

        // Load the Raphael pie chart library
    Qva.LoadScript("http://g.raphaeljs.com/g.pie.js", function() {

          Qva.AddExtension('QlikViewCookbook/RaphaelPie', function() {
    ```

```
        var _this = this;
        var vw = _this.GetWidth();
        var vh = _this.GetHeight();
        var vx = Math.floor((vw-150)/2);
        var vy = Math.floor(vh/2);
        var vr = Math.floor(0.95 * (vx > vy ? vy : vx));

        _this.Element.innerHTML = '<div id="canvas'
            + '" style="width:' + vw + 'px;'
            + 'height:' + vh + 'px;'
            + 'left: 0; position: absolute;'
            + 'top: 0;z-index:999;"></div>';

        var paper = Raphael("canvas", vw, vh);

        var dataArray = [];
        var legendValues = [];
        var colorList = ["#8DAACB",
                         "#FC7362",
                         "#BBD854",
                         "#FFD92F"];

        // Cycle Through the data
        for (var i = 0; i < _this.Data.Rows.length; i++) {
          // get the row
          var row = _this.Data.Rows [i];

          dataArray.push(parseInt(row[1].text, 10));
          legendValues.push('%%%.% ' + row[0].text);
        }

        paper.piechart(vx, vy, vr, dataArray,
            { legend: legendValues,
              colors: colorList,
              legendothers: "%%%.% Others",
              maxSlices: 3
            });

    },true);
  } );
 } );
} );
```

5. Open the QlikView document. Add a list box for the `Country` field.

6. From the **View** menu, select **Turn on/off WebView**.

7. Right-click on the sheet and select **New Sheet Object** from the menu:

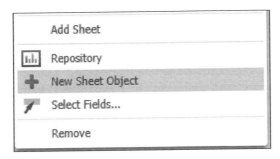

8. Click on the **Extension Objects** menu. Drag a **QlikView Cookbook Raphael** object onto the sheet. Close the **New Sheet Object** dialog.

9. Make selections in the list box and note the changes in the pie chart.

How it works...

The Raphaël library is a great example here because there are three different libraries that need to be loaded, and we can see how to nest those loads with `Qva.LoadScript`. This ensures that each of the libraries is loaded successfully before it is used.

Once the libraries are loaded, we can cycle through the `Rows` object and retrieve the values for the pie segments and the country names for the legend.

There's more...

The ability to add external libraries opens up a huge range of possibilities. jQuery is already included in QlikView 11, but you could add Raphaël, D3, JS Charts, or any of the many other libraries.

See also

▶ The *Creating an interactive extension* recipe

8
Useful Functions

In this chapter, we will cover:

- ▶ Handling null in numeric fields or calculations
- ▶ Using Dual to handle period name sorting
- ▶ Parsing text to numbers and dates
- ▶ Calculating Year To Date dynamically
- ▶ Labeling a pie chart to replace the legend
- ▶ Calculating the lowest or highest value in a range
- ▶ Consolidating a date-time value into quarter hourly segments
- ▶ Dynamically filtering by From/To dates

Introduction

QlikView has literally hundreds of functions that you can use. There are many of them which you will never use, and for some you may create some work around because you didn't know that they existed.

In this chapter, we will look at some of those functions that I think are really useful to know about and that you might never find unless you go looking for them.

Handling null in numeric fields or calculations

Whether in the QlikView script or in an expression, we often have to check if a value is null (absence of value) or blank (empty string) before using it in a calculation. SQL developers will be used to the ISNULL or COALESCE function and it is useful to have an equivalent. There is an IsNull() function in QlikView, which returns a Boolean true/false. My experience is that this does not always work reliably on all platforms and, if I want a IsNull Boolean, I tend to check Len(Field)=0 or Len(Trim(Field))=0 instead. This is a little clunky to use with an If statement in an expression so I find the Alt function to be much more elegant.

Alt can take any number of parameters and will return the first one in the list that is a number. In this case, I will only use two parameters—the field to be tested and then either 0 or 1—depending on what I want the default to be.

Getting ready

Load the following script:

```
Alt_Example:
Load * Inline [
    Month, LocalSales, ExRate
    2013-01-01, 1000, 1.1
    2013-02-01, 976,
    2013-03-01, 1100, 1.2
];
```

How to do it...

These steps show you how to handle null in numeric fields or calculations:

1. Create a straight table with Month as the dimension.Add the following three expressions:

   ```
   Sum(LocalSales)
   Sum(LocalSales * ExRate)
   Sum(LocalSales * Alt(ExRate,1))
   ```

2. Note the difference in the results.

How it works...

The `Alt` function in the third expression makes sure that a default value of `1` is applied when the exchange rate is null.

There's more...

It is important to ensure that the default value that you want is the second value in the function, otherwise that will become the first value and will override the value that you want!

When using this in the script, be sure that the value is definitely numeric or it may always be the default value. If it is numbers that are expressed as text, you can use the `num#` function to make sure that they are seen as numbers.

See also

▸ The *Parsing text to numbers and dates* recipe in this chapter

Using Dual to handle period name sorting

QlikView does not have any data types. All data is stored as dual values, a number, and a text representation. Pure text values are still stored as dual, but just the number part is null.

A common field that is created in a QlikView script is the `Month` field linked to a date. This is a great example of dual because it has a number from 1 to 12, and a text representation from January to December. However, some companies, especially in their financial applications, have periods that do not start in January. For example, it is quite common for companies in the UK to have a financial year starting in April. In this recipe, we are going to create a `Period` field that has a period number and a matching month name that does not match the calendar year and month.

How to do it...

Use the following steps to use Dual to handle period name sorting:

1. Load the following script:

```
Calendar:
Load
    Date(TempDate) As Date,
    Year(TempDate) As Year,
```

```
        Year(YearStart(TempDate, 0, 4)) As FY,
        Month(TempDate) As Month,
        Dual(
          Text(Month(TempDate)),
          Num(Month(MonthStart(TempDate, -3)))
          ) As Period,
        Date(MonthStart(TempDate), 'YYYY-MM') as YearMonth,
        Dual(
          Year(YearStart(TempDate, 0, 4)) & '-'
            & Num(Month(MonthStart(TempDate, -3)), '00'),
          MonthStart(TempDate)
          ) As FYPeriod
      ;
    Load
      RecNo()-1+Floor(MakeDate(2012)) As TempDate
    AutoGenerate(730);
```

2. Add listboxes for `Period` and `Month` onto the layout. Note that Period sorts from April to December and then from January to March.

How it works...

Creating our own dual values is as simple as using the `Dual` function and passing it in the text and numeric values that we want.

Here, we use a couple of useful date parsing functions such as `YearStart` and `MonthStart`, with parameters to allow us to offset the date to take into account the fact that we are starting our financial year in April instead of January.

There's more...

We use Dual in the script here, and in general it is better to do as much processing in the script as possible, but there is nothing to prevent you from using `Dual` in expressions or in calculated dimensions in the layout.

See also

▶ The *Labeling a pie chart to replace the legend* recipe in this chapter

Parsing text to numbers and dates

Quite often, we have to deal with data that are not in a format that QlikView can interpret as either dates or numbers. In these cases, we need to look at the data interpretation functions, `Date#` and `Num#`.

These functions accept a value and a format string. They use the format string to attempt to interpret the value.

In this recipe, we will look at using `Date#` and `Num#` functions to interpret our data correctly.

Getting ready

Load the following script:

```
Load
   Date#(Month, 'DD.MM.YYYY') As Month,
   Num#(Sales, '#.###,##', '.') As Sales
Inline [
   Month, Sales
   01.01.2013, 1.000
   01.02.2013, 976
   01.03.2013, 1.100
];
```

How to do it...

These steps show you how to parse text to numbers and dates:

1. Add a listbox for **Sales** and **Month** onto the layout:

Sales	🔎
	1.000
	1.100
	976

2. Note that the values are right-justified and that they retain the original formatting.

How it works...

The # functions apply a format string to the incoming value. If it parses correctly as number (or date) then it loads the value as a number.

There are no types in QlikView so all values are loaded as dual. The # functions will return the original value as the text portion of the dual.

There's more...

If you are faced with several formats in the same file, you can combine several # functions as parameters to an `Alt` function. The first one that returns a valid number will be the return.

It is worth remembering that the # functions, like `Date#` and `Num#`, can be confused with similarly named functions, like `Date` and `Num`, that do the opposite of what the # function does. The # functions interpret a value based on a format string, and the other functions apply a format, whereas `Date#` takes a string of text and applies a format string to interpret it as a date, the `Date` function takes a date and applies a format string to end up with a formatted string (actually a Dual value).

See also

▸ The *Handling null in numeric fields or calculations* recipe in this chapter

Calculating Year To Date dynamically

The `YearToDate` function is one of those that you might use quite often. Mostly, it will be used with default parameters, or perhaps with the offset specified. But there are a number of parameters to this function that can make it even more useful.

In this recipe, we are going to examine using the function to deal with a user entering the year end date dynamically. We will also base it off a financial year starting in April.

Getting ready

Load the following script:

```
Load
  Date(TempDate) As Date,
  Year(YearStart(TempDate, 0, 4)) As FY,
  Dual(
    Text(Month(TempDate)),
    Num(Month(MonthStart(TempDate, -3)))
    ) As Period,
  Dual(
    Year(YearStart(TempDate, 0, 4)) & '-'
      & Num(Month(MonthStart(TempDate, -3)), '00'),
    MonthStart(TempDate)
    ) As FYPeriod,
  Year(TempDate) + Month(TempDate) + Day(TempDate) As Sales
  ;
Load
  RecNo()-1+Floor(MakeDate(2012)) As TempDate
AutoGenerate(730);
```

How to do it...

Follow these steps find out how to calculate Year to Date dynamically:

1. Create a new variable called `vYEDate`. Set its initial value to `41364` (31st March 2013).

2. Add a new Bar chart with no dimension. Add the following two expressions:

Label	Expression
YTD	-Sum(Sales * YearToDate(Date, 0, 4, vYEDate))
LYTD	-Sum(Sales * YearToDate(Date, -1, 4, vYEDate))

3. Add a new Slider/Calendar object with input set to Calendar. The **Data** should be linked to the variable, **vYEDate**. Make sure that there is no **Min Value** or **Max Value** set. On the **Number** tab, select the **Override Document Settings** option and select **Date**. On the **Caption** tab, select **Show Caption** and enter `Select Year End Date` in the **Title Text**.

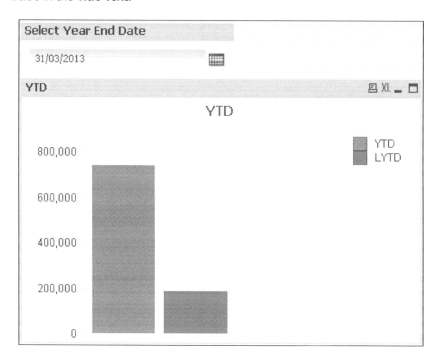

4. Note that there is a large difference between the two values. Change the Year End Date to 1st April 2013.

5. Note that the values are almost the same.

How it works...

The function has up to four parameters – only the first is mandatory. The first one is the date value that we want to test. The second parameter specifies an offset of the year that we want to compare, 0 (the default) is the year of the base date, and -1 is the previous year. The third parameter specifies what period your year starts at, 1 is January, 2 is February, and so on. The last parameter is the base date, which is the date that represents "today" for the purpose of calculating the Year To Date (defaults to today's date).

In this recipe, we pass the variable value as this base date, and the first year end that we specify is 31st March 2013. Because we have set the period value to 4, the `YearToDate` function will be based on years starting on the 1st April. So, we are comparing 1st April 2012 to 31st March 2013 versus 1st April 2011 to 31st March 2012. But our data load only starts on 1st January 2012, so the values are very different.

When we change the value to 1st April 2013, we are now comparing as if the date today was 1st April, so we are only comparing one day versus another.

`YearToDate` is a Boolean function so it returns either true or false. In QlikView, Boolean functions return 0 for false and -1 for true. That is why there is a – character at the beginning of the expressions in order to convert that negative true to a positive value.

There's more...

Performing a `Sum (FactValue * Flag)` function is very common in QlikView and quite an efficient function. It is even more efficient if the flag is calculated in the script.

Labeling a pie chart to replace the legend

Standard pie charts in QlikView suffer from a legendary problem – the legend. The problem is that the eye needs to move back and forth between the chart and the legend to help make sense of the data.

In this recipe, we are going to remove the legend and use the Dual function to replace it with text besides each segment that identifies the information.

Getting ready

Load the following script:

```
LOAD * INLINE [
    Country, Sales
    USA, 1000
    Mexico, 600
    Canada, 700
    UK, 900
    Germany, 800
];
```

How to do it...

These steps show you how to label a pie chart to replace the legend:

1. Create a pie chart with `Country` as the dimension. Add the following expression:

    ```
    =Dual (
      if(Len(Only(Country))>0, Country, 'Others')
      & chr(10) & Num(Sum(Sales), '#,##0')
      ,Sum(Sales)
      )
    ```

2. On the **Expression** tab, label the expression as `Sales $` and turn on the **Values on Data Points** option.

3. On the **Sort** tab, turn on the **Y-Value** option.

4. On the **Presentation** tab, turn off the **Show Legend** option.

5. On the **Numbers** tab, ensure that **Expression Default** is selected.

6. Click on **OK** to save the chart. Note that the country names and values are displayed besides each segment.

7. Edit the properties of the chart. On the **Dimension Limits** tab, turn on the **Restrict which values...** option and set the **Show only** option to **Largest** and enter 4 for the **Values**:

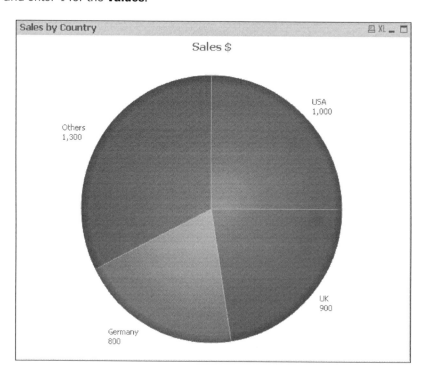

How it works...

The `Dual` function takes a text value and a numeric value. For the text value, we are providing the country name and the formatted sales value with a line feed of `chr(10)` to wrap the text. The numeric sales value is what QlikView uses to calculate the size of the segments. The text value is displayed by the **Values on Data Points** option.

It is important here that the **Number** option be always **Expression Default**. If you were to choose a different option, then that would override the text from the dual and just present the formatted number.

It is never a good idea to display more than a few segments in a pie chart, so we restrict the number to four and our expression handles there being more than one country by testing with the `Only()` function.

The `Only()` function is interesting here as it only returns a value if there is only one value to return. In fact, it is not necessary in the expression because if you use a field name like this, without an aggregation, there is an implied `Only()` and it will be null if there is more than one value or no values.

There's more...

This method of using `Dual` can be applied to many other charts. We could also include the **Text as Pop-up** option in the **Expression** tab and turn off the **Pop-up labels** in the **Presentation** tab to get this text become the hover-over display.

See also

▶ The *Using Dual to handle period name sorting* recipe in this chapter

Calculating the lowest or highest value in a range

It is quite often useful for us to calculate the lowest or highest value in a range. There are possibilities to do this using `AGGR`, but within a chart we can also make use of the Range functions along with some of the chart inter-record functions, such as `Above`, `Below`, `Before`, `After`, `First`, `Last`, and so on.

In this recipe, we are going to calculate the highest and lowest values in a range so that we can assign a relative color to them using the `ColorMix1` function.

Load the following script:

```
LOAD * INLINE [
     Country, Sales
     USA, 1100
     Mexico, 650
     Canada, 709
     UK, 932
     Germany, 800
     France, 777
     Australia, 537
     Japan, 898
     Russia, 687
];
```

How to do it...

Follow these steps to find out how to calculate the lowest or highest value in a range:

1. Create a Block chart. Add `Country` as the dimension. Add the following expression:

   `Sum(Sales)`

2. Click on the **+** sign besides the expression and enter the following expression for the **Background**:

   ```
   ColorMix1(
   (Sum(Sales)
   -RangeMin(
     Above(Sum(Sales), 0, RowNo()),
     Below(Sum(Sales), 1, NoOfRows()-RowNo())
     ))
   /
   (RangeMax(
     Above(Sum(Sales), 0, RowNo()),
     Below(Sum(Sales), 1, NoOfRows()-RowNo())
     )
   -RangeMin(
     Above(Sum(Sales), 0, RowNo()),
     Below(Sum(Sales), 1, NoOfRows()-RowNo())
     ))
   , White(), LightBlue())
   ```

3. Click on **OK** to save the chart. Note the variation in color of the blocks.

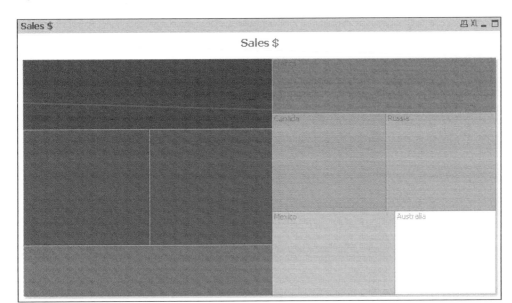

How it works...

The chart inter-record functions look at the values of expression around the current cell. For example, the Above(Sum(Sales)) expression will return what the value of the Sum(Sales) expression is in the cell immediately above the current cell. We can pass additional parameters to the Above function. The second parameter is the start position, which defaults to 1. The third parameter is the number of rows to return. This also defaults to 1 and that returns only 1 value. If there is more than one row then we need to use a Range function to handle the values.

By passing the value of 0 as the start row and using the RowNo() function as the number of rows, the Above function returns all the values up to the current row.

The Below function works similarly, but returns rows below the current row. We pass it the value 1 as the start position to the row immediately below the current one, and then calculate the number of rows to use as the total number of rows, given by NoOfRows(), minus the current row, given by RowNo().

So, on each row of the chart, we are using both Above and Below to pass the range of values through to the RangeMax and RangeMin functions.

There's more...

AGGR could have been used here, but these functions used the cached calculated values from the chart itself so should be more efficient. Use AGGR when the calculation is something different to the one being calculated in the chart.

Consolidating a date-time value into quarter hourly segments

Databases quite often capture date and time information to the millisecond in TimeStamp fields. However, it is rare that you will need to analyze this information to the millisecond or even to the minute. In fact, for the vast majority of implementations, we would only analyze to the day – or even higher.

If you do need to analyze time slices during a day, it would be rare to go down to the minute, mostly it would be to the hour. But it might want to go to the quarter hour. There is some debate on what minutes go into a quarter-hour slice, but I take a mathematical approach (time is a continuous numeric value) to this and use the Round function. Therefore, 11:58 would appear under 12:00 and 12:08 would go to 12:15.

Getting ready

Load the following script:

```
Load
  TimeCounter,
  Date(TimeStamp) as Date,
  WeekDay(TimeStamp) As WeekDay,
  TimeStamp(Round(TimeStamp, (1/(24))), 'M/D/YY HH:mm') As Hour,
  TimeStamp(Round(TimeStamp, (1/(24*4))), 'M/D/YY HH:mm')
As QuarterHour;
Load
  Today() + (Rand()) As TimeStamp,
  1 as TimeCounter
AutoGenerate(1000);
```

How to do it...

To consolidate a date-time value into quarter hour segments, follow these steps:

1. Add a Line chart to the document with `QuarterHour` as its dimension. Add the following expression:

    `Sum(TimeCounter)`

2. Note that the data is displayed in quarter-hour chunks:

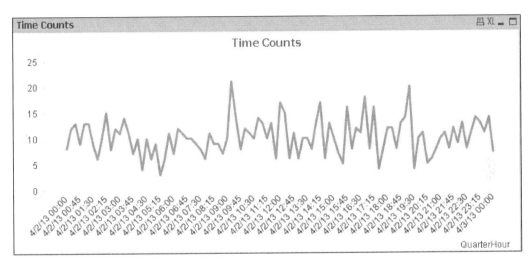

How it works...

The `Round` function in QlikView is very different from that in many other script or development languages. Usually, a `Round` function takes as a parameter the number of decimal places to round to. In QlikView, the parameter is the value to round to the nearest. So, if we gave it a value of 1, it would round to the nearest integer. If we gave it 0.1, then it would round to the nearest one-tenth. But we could equally give it a value of five and it would round to the nearest multiple of five.

In this example, we are giving two values – 1/24 (0.04167) and 1/24*4 (0.0104167). These seem like strange values until we think in terms of time. Time is stored as a fraction of 1 day so 1/24 is 1 hour. 1/24*4 is 1 quarter hour. By using these values with QlikView's `Round` function, we get our Date/Time value rounded as required.

There's more...

By rounding time stamp values in this manner, we are increasing the efficiency of our QlikView document. This is because time stamps tend to be highly unique, taking up a lot of memory space, whereas the rounded values will have much fewer repeating values which works well with QlikView's columnar storage.

Dynamically filtering by From/To dates

Quite often, users who are not quite familiar with the QlikView way of making selections, will ask for a From/To date selection option that they are used to from their previous reporting solutions.

We can do this using a couple of variables and an Action applied to a button.

Getting ready

Load the following script:

```
Load
   Date(TempDate) As Date,
   Year(TempDate) As Year,
   Month(TempDate) As Month,
   Date(MonthStart(TempDate), 'YYYY-MM') As YearMonth,
   (Year(TempDate) + Month(TempDate) + Day(TempDate)) * Rand() As Sales
   ;
Load
   RecNo()-1+Floor(MakeDate(2012)) As TempDate
AutoGenerate(730);
```

How to do it...

These steps will show you how to dynamically filter by From/To dates:

1. Add a new variable to the `vStartDate` document with a value of `41275` (1st January 2013 – no particular reason for this value).

2. Add a new variable to the `vEndDate` document with a value of `41364` (31st March 2013).

3. Create a new Line chart with dimensions of `Month` and `Year`. Add the following expression:

   ```
   Sum(Sales)
   ```

4. Add a new Slider/Calendar object with input set to Calendar. The **Data** should be linked to the variable, **vStartDate**. Make sure that there is no **Min Value** or **Max Value** set. On the **Number** tab, select the **Override Document Settings** option and select **Date**. On the Caption tab, select **Show Caption** and enter `Select From Date` in the **Title Text**.

5. Add a new Slider/Calendar object with input set to Calendar. The **Data** should be linked to the variable, **vEndDate**. Make sure that there is no **Min Value** or **Max Value** set. On the **Number** tab, select the **Override Document Settings** option and select **Date**. On the Caption tab, select **Show Caption** and enter `Select To Date` in the **Title Text**.

6. Add a new Current Selections box to the layout. Accept the default options.

7. Add a new listbox for the `Date` field.

8. Add a new Button object to the layout. The **Text** should be set to **Apply**.

9. On the button's **Action** tab, click on the **Add** button. Select **Selection** for the **Action Type** and **Select in Field** for the **Action**. Click on **OK**.

10. Enter `Date` for the **Field**. Enter the following expression for the **Search String**:

    ```
    ='>=' & Date(vStartDate) & '<=' & Date(vEndDate)
    ```

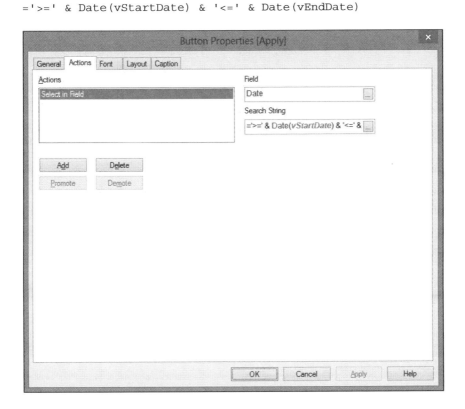

11. Click **OK** to save the button.

12. Select different dates in the calendar boxes and see what happens when you click the button.

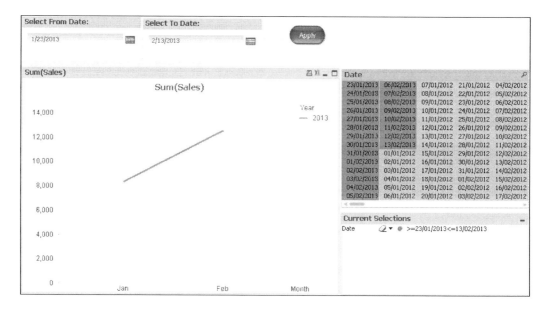

How it works...

The magic here is in the Action and in the expression that is being used to calculate the search string.

We store the variables as numbers because they are easier to deal with, but we then apply the `date` function to format them as dates into a format that the `Date` field will accept. If the `Date` field was in a different format, we would need to add that format string to the function, otherwise the expression would fail.

There's more...

Using Actions to apply selections are a common enough thing to do. However, I would caution that it should not be done without the user being aware of it, and you should always include a Current Selections box so that they can see what has happened.

9
Script

In this chapter, we will cover the following recipes:

- ▸ Creating flags in the script
- ▸ Replacing IsNull
- ▸ Storing and dropping using a subroutine
- ▸ Keeping a trace on things
- ▸ Using the AND mode in listboxes
- ▸ Using Exists and Keep to limit the data load
- ▸ Setting the default display format
- ▸ Setting the default sort order
- ▸ Matching financial periods to dates
- ▸ Handling partial reload in the script
- ▸ Using Peek and Previous to calculate against loaded records
- ▸ Creating a simple Gantt for a dashboard using Interval Match
- ▸ Reading users from Active Directory
- ▸ Getting a sub-URL using the Table wizard
- ▸ Using parameters in Dollar Sign Expansion
- ▸ Removing fields with a wildcard
- ▸ Handling multiple subfolders in a script

Introduction

This chapter is all about the QlikView script. QlikView script is the place where we tell QlikView how to load data into memory. I will assume that as a part of whatever training or self-teaching you have had, you will have learned how to write QlikView scripts.

It is one thing to know how to load data into QlikView, it is another thing to know how to load data into QlikView so that your charts calculate correctly and quickly.

This chapter builds upon your existing knowledge and shows several tips and tricks that will make your life easier.

Creating flags in the script

Creating flags in the script is something that experienced QlikView developers will do almost without thinking. If they need to improve the performance of an expression, or just make an expression easier to write, they will probably create a flag field in the script. By moving linear calculations to the script and creating numeric fields, it means that the frontend performance will be vastly improved.

Often, these will be created by simple `If` statements, but they can also be more complex.

In this recipe, we will look at creating a flag to help us calculate the end of period positions.

Getting ready

Load the following script:

```
Load
   Date(TempDate) As Date,
   WeekDay(TempDate) as WeekDay,
   Year(TempDate) As Year,
   Month(TempDate) As Month,
   Date(MonthStart(TempDate), 'YYYY-MM') As YearMonth,
   WeekYear(TempDate) & '-'
      & Num(Week(TempDate), '00') As YearWeek,
   Floor(5000 * Rand()) As StockVolume;
Load
   RecNo()-1+Floor(MakeDate(2012)) As TempDate
AutoGenerate(730);
```

How to do it...

Follow these steps to create flags in the script:

1. Edit the QlikView script by adding the highlighted code between the `YearWeek` and `StockVolume` lines:

    ```
    . . .
      WeekYear(TempDate) & '-'
        & Num(Week(TempDate), '00') As YearWeek,
      if(TempDate = Floor(MonthEnd(TempDate)), 1, 0)
        As End_of_Month_Flag,
      if(WeekDay(TempDate) = 5, 1, 0)
        As End_of_Week_Flag,
      Floor(5000 * Rand()) As StockVolume;
    . . .
    ```

2. Reload the script.

3. Add a line chart with **YearMonth** as the dimension. Add the following expression:

    ```
    Sum({<End_of_Month_Flag={1}>} StockVolume)
    ```

4. Add another line chart with **YearWeek** as the dimension. Add the following expression:

    ```
    Sum({<End_of_Week_Flag={1}>} StockVolume)
    ```

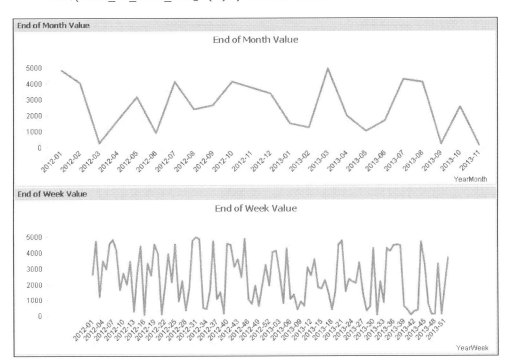

Note that your charts will look different as the values are random.

5. Add a straight table with **Date** and **Weekday** as the dimensions. Add the same two expressions as the preceding ones to this chart:

Stock Volumes			
Date	WeekDay	End of Month Volume	End of Week Volume
		58,568	246,494
07/01/2012	Sat	0	2,587
14/01/2012	Sat	0	4,698
21/01/2012	Sat	0	1,189
28/01/2012	Sat	0	3,490
31/01/2012	Tue	4,865	0
04/02/2012	Sat	0	2,971
11/02/2012	Sat	0	4,584
18/02/2012	Sat	0	4,813
25/02/2012	Sat	0	4,151
29/02/2012	Wed	4,040	0
03/03/2012	Sat	0	1,638
10/03/2012	Sat	0	2,679
17/03/2012	Sat	0	1,979
24/03/2012	Sat	0	3,450
31/03/2012	Sat	273	273
07/04/2012	Sat	0	2,744
14/04/2012	Sat	0	4,420
21/04/2012	Sat	0	33
28/04/2012	Sat	0	3,332
30/04/2012	Mon	1,707	0
05/05/2012	Sat	0	2,559
12/05/2012	Sat	0	4,517
19/05/2012	Sat	0	3,912
26/05/2012	Sat	0	86

Note that only Saturdays or month end dates have entries.

How it works...

The flags are really easy to calculate by using QlikView's built-in date functions. Once they are created in the script, it is a really simple matter to use them in a set. Creating the flags in the script makes this calculation really quick.

The WeekDay function returns a number between 0 and 6, where 0 is Monday. That is why we look for 5; which means Saturday.

There's more...

The more complex the calculation is, the more reason there is to put the calculation into the script. The simpler the calculation on the frontend, the quicker the application will respond.

This approach is very often used for such values as Invoice Paid and Ticket Closed.

Replacing IsNull

IsNull is a function that has similarities in many programming languages. It is not always the same though. In QlikView, this function returns a Boolean value of true or false; if the passed value is null.

There is a big "however" here though. Depending upon the version of QlikView that you have, IsNull does not always return what you expect. There are differences between 32-bit and 64-bit versions on how the values are handled. It should also be noted that blank values in text files or inline data will be treated as empty strings rather than null.

SQL Server developers will be familiar with the SQL function of ISNULL (or COALESCE) that, instead of just returning a Boolean value, will return a default value if the passed value is actually null. It can be useful to replicate this.

Getting ready

Load the following script:

```
Load
  Country,
  If(IsNull(Sales), 0, Sales) As Sales
Inline [
  Country, Sales
  USA, 1020
  UK,  965
  Germany,
  France, 890
];
```

How to do it...

These steps show you how to use `Alt` to replace `IsNull`:

1. Add a **Table Box** control to the layout with **Country** and **Sales** as the fields. Note that the **Sales** value for **Germany** is blank, even though the `IsNull` function has been used to test for `null`.

2. Change the `If` statement in the script to the following:

   ```
   If(Len(Trim(Sales))=0, 0, Sales) As Sales
   ```

3. Reload and note that the sales value for **Germany** is now `0`.

4. Change the **If** statement again, to the following:

   ```
   Alt(Sales, 0) As Sales
   ```

5. Reload and note that all values are now `0`! Modify the `If` statement to the following:

   ```
   Alt(Num#(Sales, '#####'), 0) As Sales
   ```

6. Reload and note that all countries now have a **Sales** value and **Germany** is `0`.

How it works...

The `If` statement using `Len` is one that I would use quite often to test for `null`. This also has the advantage of matching zero-length strings as well as `null`.

The `Alt` function is useful because it returns the first numeric value in a list. In this case, the **Sales** value was not initially recognized as being numeric; this is because the `INLINE` function returns the text by default. By applying the `Num#` function, we make sure that `Alt` knows that the values are numeric. Numeric field data from a database connection will always be interpreted as numeric and shouldn't need the conversion function, but might need `Alt`.

There's more...

When using the `Len` function, I might sometimes use a `Trim` function to clean potential spaces at the same time.

Storing and dropping using a subroutine

Loading a table of data, storing it to a QVD file, and then dropping the table, is quite a common use case. If your data strategy requires you to create a QVD layer, you will do this a lot. Whenever you need to do something more than once, it is useful to create a script subroutine and then just call it.

Getting ready

Load the following script:

```
Table1:
Load * Inline [
   Country, Sales
   USA, 1020
   UK, 965
   Germany, 1109
   France, 890
];

Table2:
Load * Inline [
   Country, Costs
   USA, 760
   UK, 545
   Germany, 879
   France, 678
];
```

How to do it...

Follow these steps to create a subroutine to store QVD then drop a table:

1. Before the `load` statement for `Table1`, add the following script:

   ```
   Sub StoreAndDrop(vTableName)
      Store [$(vTableName)] into [$(vTableName).qvd];
      Drop Table [$(vTableName)];

   End Sub
   ```

2. After the `Table1` load and before the `Table2` load, add the following line of script:

   ```
   Call StoreAndDrop('Table1');
   ```

3. After the `Table2` load, add the following line of script:

   ```
   Call StoreAndDrop('Table2');
   ```

4. Reload the script. There should be no data in the document and two QVD files should have been created in the same folder as the QVW file.

How it works...

There isn't anything too difficult involved in this. We pass a text value to the subroutine, which is the table name and then we use that value to store the table to the QVD file of the same name and then drop the table.

There's more...

Subroutines like this can be created in an external file and then included in the script (in the editor, go to **Insert | Include Statement**). This allows you to have a library of useful functions that you might use in multiple applications.

We can also add some error checking to make sure that the table name is valid:

```
Sub StoreAndDrop(vTableName)

  let vNoFields = NoOfFields('$(vTableName)');
  if Len('$(vNoFields)') > 0 Then
    Store [$(vTableName)] into [$(vTableName).qvd];
    Drop Table [$(vTableName)];
  Else
    Trace ** Cannot Store - $(vTableName) does not exist.;
  End if

End Sub
```

The `store` statement doesn't need to be just the table name; we can add other items, either static or variable:

```
Store [$(vTableName)] into [$(vQVDPath)\E_$(vTableName).qvd];
```

See also

▸ The *Keeping a trace on things* recipe in this chapter

Keeping a trace on things

When writing scripts, especially when getting into more advanced structures such as `For` or `For Each` loops, it can be important to see what is going on in the script.

The `Trace` statement allows us to write information to the Script Execution Dialog, which gives immediate feedback on what is going on, so that we can quickly diagnose issues.

Getting ready

Load the following script:

```
For i = -10 to 10

  Let vTemp = $(i) / If($(i)=-10, 1, Peek('X'));

  Data:
  Load
    $(i) As X,
    Round($(vTemp), 0.001) As Y
  AutoGenerate(1);

Next
```

How to do it...

These steps show you how to use `Trace` to write to the Script Execution Dialog:

1. Add a table box with fields `X` and `Y`.

2. The script loaded with errors. We have had errors and we are not getting the correct result. Add the following line of script after the `Let` statement:

   ```
   Trace On row $(i), the result is $(vTemp);
   ```

3. Reload the script:

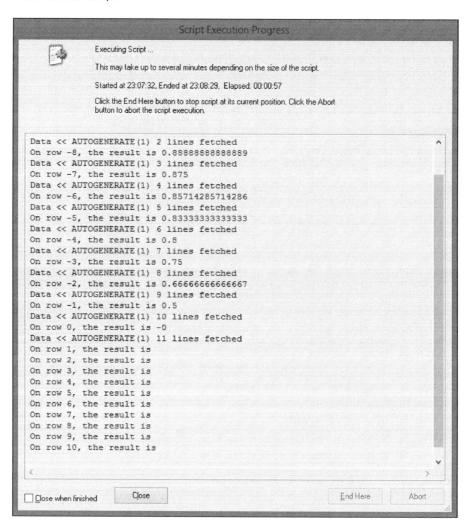

Note that the first failure occurs on row 1 and all other rows after that fail.

4. Change the script to allow for other zero values causing a `null` response:

```
For i = -10 to 10

    Let vTemp = Alt($(i) / Peek('X'), 0);

    Trace On row $(i), the result is $(vTemp);
```

```
    Data:
    Load
      $(i) As X,
      Round($(vTemp), 0.001) As Y
    AutoGenerate(1);

  Next
```

5. Reload and note that the script now executes.

How it works...

Just by having more information about what row the error started happening upon, we can solve the problem quickly.

The `Trace` statement allows us to combine static text and variable values to output to the script execution dialog. The variable values are added using the dollar sign expansion mechanism.

There's more...

Lines written to the script execution dialog will also be written to the log file if logging is turned on.

The **Debug** option in **Script Editor** is another good way of tracking what is happening during execution, especially when dollar sign expansion is used.

See also

▸   The *Replacing IsNull* recipe in this chapter

Using the AND mode in listboxes

The default mode for listbox selection is OR. When we select more than one value in a listbox, the selection is `value1`, `value2`, or `value3`. There will be occasions where we will want the selection to be AND—show us results which are linked `to value1` AND `value2` AND `value3`.

This is possible in QlikView, but we have to set up the data in a particular way.

Getting ready

We will be using the Movies Database demo QlikView document as a source for this example. There should be a copy installed by the default installation of QlikView 11 into your **Program Files** folders. You can also download it from `http://demo.qlikview.com`.

1. Create a new QlikView document and save it. Edit the script and remove all the default added text (`SET` statements).

2. Click on the QlikView **File ...** button and browse to the `Movies Database.qvw` file. This should add a statement similar to the following to your script:

   ```
   Binary [c:\program files\qlikview\examples\documents\movies
   database.qvw];
   ```

3. Reload the document; this will load all of the data from the `Movies qvw` into your document.

How to do it...

These steps show you how to use AND mode in listboxes:

1. Add a listbox for `Actor` and one for `Title`. Edit the properties of the `Title` listbox and set the title to the following expression:

   ```
   =Count(DISTINCT Title)
   ```

2. Select **Elizabeth Taylor** in the **Actor** listbox. Hold down the *Ctrl* key and select **Richard Burton**:

3. Note that 102 movies are listed in the **Title** listbox. This is all the movies that have either **Elizabeth Taylor** or **Richard Burton** in them. We would like to see the movies that have both the actors.

4. Edit the script. After the `Binary` statement, add the following script:

```
ANDActors:
Load Distinct
    FilmID,
    Actor as ANDActor
Resident
    Actors;
```

5. Reload the script and clear the current selections.

6. Edit the properties of the **Actors** listbox and select **ANDActor** in the **Field** drop-down list. Click on **OK** and then edit the properties again. Turn on the **And Mode** checkbox, then click on **OK** again.

7. Select **Elizabeth Taylor** again. Note the **&** that appears beside her name. Also note that not all the other values have been grayed out.

8. Again, hold down the *Ctrl* key and select **Richard Burton**. Both values should have an **&** beside them. Note that only 10 movies are listed.

9. Hold down the *Ctrl* key and click, but hold for a couple of seconds on **Michael Hordern**. Instead of **&**, the actor should get an **!**, and instead of being green, the selection should be red:

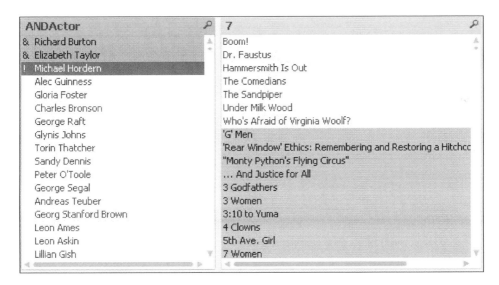

10. Note that only seven movies are listed. This is all of the movies that starred both **Elizabeth Taylor** and **Richard Burton** but did not star **Michael Hordern**.

How it works...

The magic here is the way the **ANDActor** table is loaded. The first rule is that this table can only have two fields, one of which is the key field that links the table to the data (`FilmID` here) and the other is the field that we are going to use in the listbox.

The second rule is that this table must be loaded with the `Distinct` keyword so that only unique combinations of fields are loaded.

Once the table is loaded in this fashion, the **And Mode** checkbox, which is usually grayed out, becomes available.

There's more...

It is rare that you will need to use this functionality. For the majority of use cases, the OR mode selection is exactly what is needed.

Using Exists and Keep to limit the data load

Quite often, we need to restrict the amount of data that we are loading. We can usually do this by comparing the value in a particular field to some other value (for example, `Year > 2010`), but we might also need to load the data based on the values that have already been loaded into memory.

Getting ready

Load the following script:

```
Sales:
LOAD * INLINE [
  Year, Country, SalesPersonID, Sales
  2011, Germany, 1, 1233
  2012, Germany, 1, 2133
  2013, Germany, 1, 3421
  2011, UK, 2, 1567
  2012, UK, 2, 2244
  2013, UK, 2, 2567
  2011, USA, 3, 1098
  2012, USA, 3, 1123
  2013, USA, 3, 1456
];
```

```
SalesPerson:
LOAD SPID As SalesPersonID,
   SalesPersonName as SalesPerson;
Load * INLINE [
   SPID, SalesPersonName
   1, John Smith
   2, Jayne Volta
   3, Graham Brown
   4, Anita Weisz
];

Budget:
LOAD * INLINE [
   Year, Country, Budget
   2012, Germany, 2100
   2013, Germany, 3100
   2014, Germany, 4100
   2012, UK, 2100
   2013, UK, 2600
   2014, UK, 3100
   2012, USA, 1100
   2013, USA, 1200
   2014, USA, 1300
];
```

How to do it...

These steps show you how to use `Exists` and `Keep` to limit the data load:

1. Add a listbox for `Year` and one for `SalesPerson`. Note that there are four values in each. However, there is one extra sales person that we don't need at this time. There is also a year's budget that we don't need to include. Modify the `SalesPerson` table load as follows:

   ```
   SalesPerson:
   LOAD SPID As SalesPersonID,
      SalesPersonName as SalesPerson
   Where Exists(SalesPersonID, SPID);
   Load * INLINE [
      SPID, SalesPersonName
      1, John Smith
      2, Jayne Volta
   ```

```
    3, Graham Brown
    4, Anita Weisz
];
```

2. Modify the `Budget` load as follows:

```
Budget:
Left Keep (Sales)
LOAD * INLINE [
    Year, Country, Budget
    2012, Germany, 2100
    2013, Germany, 3100
    2014, Germany, 4100
    2012, UK, 2100
    2013, UK, 2600
    2014, UK, 3100
    2012, USA, 1100
    2013, USA, 1200
    2014, USA, 1300
];
```

3. Reload the script and note that each listbox only has three values. Open the table viewer and note that the budget is still a separate table.

4. Modify the `Keep` statement for the `Budget` load to the following:

```
Inner Keep (Sales)
```

5. Reload and note that there are now only two values in the **Year** listbox.

How it works...

The `Exists` clause on the `SalesPerson` load checks to see if the value being loaded (`SPID`) already exists in the already loaded data (`SalesPersonID`). If it does, then the sales person gets loaded.

The `Keep` clause acts in a similar way to a `Join` statement, except that the tables are not joined. Rows in the tables are only kept if they match the join. In the first case, we use a Left Keep so the data in the `Sales` table is all retained and we just don't load the budget data that doesn't match. In the second case, (the Inner Keep), both tables lose the records that don't match an Inner.

There's more...

`Exists` is also useful to load the data that doesn't already exist by using the `Not` operator—`Where Not Exists(...)`.

If there is only one field between two tables, then either `Exists` or `Keep` can be used. If there is more than one, then `Keep` may be easier. However, it should be noted that `Exists` does not always need to use key fields as the second parameter to the `Exists` function can be an expression.

Setting the default display format

The default document format for a numeric value (the text part of the dual value) is decided on by QlikView when the field is first loaded. This can be a problem if the incoming data is unclean, or you want to change the format as it is loaded.

The usual approach is to use one of the formatting functions, like `Num` or `Date`, to apply the format as it is being loaded. This can be troublesome if you are loading from QVD and want to retain the QVD optimization on loading—adding a `Num` or `Date` function would lose that optimized load.

There is another way. In this recipe, we can see that by loading the data in a temporary table first, we can force the format for the rest of the data.

Getting ready

Load the following script:

```
Data:
Load * Inline [
  Date, Value
  2013-01-01, 1234.56
  2013-01-14, 3245
  2013-03-12, 2389.6
];


Store Data into Data.qvd;

Drop Table Data;

Data:
Load * From Data.qvd (QVD);
```

How to do it...

These steps show you how to set a default display format:

1. Add a listbox for `Date` and one for `Value`. Note that they default to the format of the incoming data.

2. Add the following script after the `Drop Table` statement and before the second `Load` statement:

```
Temp1:
Load
   Date(Today(), 'M/D/YYYY') As Date
AutoGenerate(1);

Temp2:
Load
   Num(0, '#,##0.00') As Value
AutoGenerate(1);
```

3. Add the following code to the end of the script, after the `Load` statement:

```
Drop Tables Temp1, Temp2;
```

4. Reload the data.

5. Note that the fields are formatted with the format string that we specified.

How it works...

QlikView doesn't really work with tables as an SQL developer might think, it really only deals with fields (columns). When we loaded the `Date` and `Value` fields in the temp tables, and then loaded a `Date` and `Value` fields from the QVD; as far as QlikView is concerned, there is only the one `Date` field and one `Value` field. When we formatted the fields with just one format string, it sets the default format for all subsequent loads. We then clean up the dummy data at the end by dropping the tables; this removes all the non-associated data.

There's more...

We could have loaded the dummy data; in this case, in just one table. However, as the actual data only had the same two fields, there would have been an automatic concatenation.

See also

▶ The *Setting the default sort order* recipe in this chapter

Setting the default sort order

The sort order of a field will usually default to numeric or text order. Sometimes, this is not what we want because neither may be appropriate for a particular field. We can use a custom sort based on an expression but that adds an additional overhead to the frontend.

The most performant sort is the **Load Order** sort option. However, we cannot always rely on the order in which that data may have been loaded.

In this recipe, we will show how we can default that sort order.

Getting ready

Load the following script:

```
Data:
LOAD * INLINE [
    Country, Rank
    France, Low
    Ireland, Low
    Germany, High
    USA, High
    UK, Med
    Japan, Med
];
```

How to do it...

Follow these steps to set a default sort order:

1. Add a listbox for `Country` and one for `Rank`. Note that `Rank` defaults to a `High`, `Low`, or **Medium** text order.

2. Edit the script. Before the data table load, add the following code:

```
Temp:
Load * INLINE [
    Rank
    High
    Med
    Low
];
```

3. After the data table load, add the following code:

```
Drop Table Temp;
```

4. Reload the script. Modify the properties of the **Rank** listbox and on the **Sort** tab, set the **Sort by** option to **Load Order**.

5. Note that the data displays as **High**, **Med**, or **Low**.

How it works...

By loading the dummy table, we are preloading that field in a particular order. When QlikView loads the additional data, it doesn't add the new data; just tags the existing data as being associated with **Country**. When we call the Drop Table, the data doesn't get dropped; just disassociated with the Temp table.

It is important to note that the dummy table should be dropped after, not before, all the other data is loaded, or the sort order may be lost.

There's more...

You can have one SortOrder table at the beginning of your load script, and then concatenate new data fields as you need them.

See also

▸ The *Setting the default display format* recipe in this chapter

Matching financial periods to dates

It would be a wonderful world if all companies had their financial year starting on the 1st of January, and each financial period matched to a calendar month. But that isn't the case, and companies often start their year on different dates and have different financial periods across their year.

In this recipe, we will look at a company that uses periods based on weeks that do not exactly match to months. We have a table that defines the start and end of each period, and we need to map that to our calendar.

Getting ready

Load the following script:

```
PeriodTable:
LOAD * INLINE [
    PeriodNumber, PeriodStart, PeriodEnd
    1, 2013-01-01, 2013-01-27
    2, 2013-01-28, 2013-02-24
    3, 2013-02-25, 2013-03-31
    4, 2013-04-01, 2013-04-28
    5, 2013-04-29, 2013-05-26
    6, 2013-05-27, 2013-06-30
    7, 2013-07-01, 2013-07-28
    8, 2013-07-29, 2013-08-25
    9, 2013-08-26, 2013-09-29
    10, 2013-09-30, 2013-10-27
    11, 2013-10-28, 2013-11-24
    12, 2013-11-25, 2013-12-31
];

Calendar:
Load
    TempDate as DateID,
    Date(TempDate) As Date,
    Day(TempDate) As Day,
    Month(TempDate) As Month,
    Year(TempDate) As Year;
Load
    RecNo()-1+Floor(MakeDate(2013)) As TempDate
AutoGenerate(365);
```

How to do it...

The following steps show you how to match financial periods to dates:

1. Add a listbox for `PeriodNumber` and one for `Date`. Note that selections on either do not affect the other as they are not currently associated.

2. Add the following code to the end of the script and reload:

    ```
    Link:
    IntervalMatch(DateID)
    ```

```
Load
   PeriodStart,
   PeriodEnd
Resident
   PeriodTable;
```

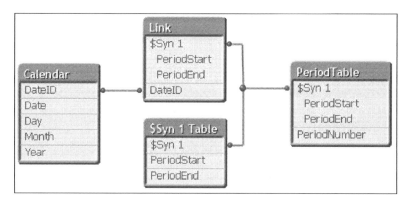

3. Selections on `PeriodNumber` should now affect the `Date` field. But there is a synthetic key in this structure, and the "best practice" recommendation is that we should remove it. Add the following script:

```
Left Join (Link)
Load
   PeriodStart,
   PeriodEnd,
   PeriodNumber
Resident
   PeriodTable;

Left Join (Calendar)
Load
   DateID,
   PeriodNumber
Resident
   Link;

Drop Table Link;
```

4. Reload and note that the synthetic key has gone.

How it works...

The `IntervalMatch` function creates a table that will link the start and end values to the `DateID` value. We can then join the `PeriodNumber` value into this link table and finally join that data into `Calendar` and drop the link table.

There's more...

There is also an advanced syntax for the period match, which allows you to match both a period and additional keys.

See also

► The *Creating a simple Gantt for a dashboard using Interval Match* recipe in this chapter

Handling partial reload in the script

Partial reload in QlikView allows us to add additional data into some tables while leaving other tables alone. This can be great if you have transactional information that you reload quite frequently and you want to minimize the load time. We can add the additional data without having to reload everything else.

In this recipe, we will see how to use the `IsPartialReload` function to handle partial reloads.

Getting ready

Load the following script:

```
Static:
Load
   RowNo() As ID1,
   'Static' As DataType1,
   Timestamp(Now()) As TimeStamp1
AutoGenerate(1);

Dynamic:
Load
   RowNo() As ID2,
   'Dynamic1' As DataType2,
   Timestamp(Now()) As TimeStamp2
AutoGenerate(1);
```

How to do it...

These steps show you how to handle partial reload in the script:

1. Add two table boxes. The first should have `ID1`, `DataType1`, and `TimeStamp1`. The second should have `ID2`, `DataType2`, and `TimeStamp2`. There should be one row in each.

2. Add the following code at the end of the script:

```
If IsPartialReload() Then

    Dynamic:
    Add
    Load
        RowNo() As ID2,
        'Dynamic2' As DataType2,
        Timestamp(Now()) As TimeStamp2
    AutoGenerate(1);

End If
```

3. From the **File** menu, select **Partial Reload** (*Ctrl + Shift + R*). Note that the second table box now has additional data, while the first has not changed.

4. Modify the script and change the following code:

```
Add
```

to

```
Replace
```

5. Do a normal reload and then a partial reload. Note that the first table box retains the values from the normal reload. The second table box still has only one row, but the time stamp has updated.

How it works...

The `Add` statement in the load indicates to QlikView that it should add the additional rows to the existing table. The **Replace** function will drop the existing table and replace it.

Wrapping `Add` or `Replace` in the `IsPartialReload` test makes sure that they only get called during a partial reload. The statements outside `IsPartialReload` will not be executed during a partial reload.

There's more...

The `IsPartialReload` test is also useful to check if it is not a partial reload; you might want to do something completely different!

Using Peek and Previous to calculate against loaded records

`Previous` is an excellent function to be able to use in a QlikView script, because it allows us to look back at previous source records. `Peek` allows us to look at records that have already been loaded into memory.

Both are very useful for making vertical calculations in the script. In this recipe, we will look at making period-on-period calculations.

Getting ready

Go to `http://www.bls.gov/lau/`, and look for the **County Data** table. Download the text file (currently at `http://www.bls.gov/lau/laucntycur14.txt`) to your PC.

Follow these steps to load the data:

1. Edit the script and click on the **Table Files** button:

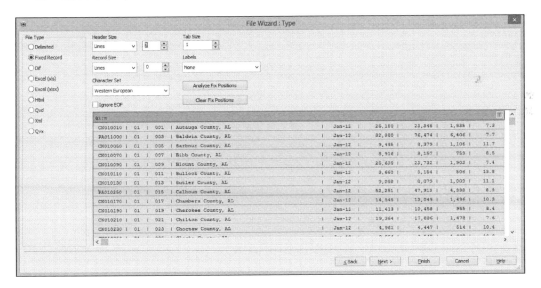

2. Browse to the file that we downloaded previously. Set the **File Type** to **Fixed Record**. Set **Record Size** to **Lines**. Set **Header Size** also to **Lines,** and then increase the number of rows until all the header rows (including dashes) are removed:

@102:113		@114:n	
23,345	||	1,835 |	7.3
76,474	|'	6,406 |	7.7
8,379	||	1,106 |	11.7
8,157	||	759 |	8.5
23,732	|,	115 |	7.4
3,154	||	506 |	13.8
8,079	|'	1,009 |	11.1
47,913	||	4,338 |	8.3
13,049	||	1,496 |	10.3
10,458	|,	955 |	8.4
17,886	||	1,478 |	7.6
4,447	|'	514 |	10.4

3. Click on either side of each of the bars (**|**) in the text to create the correct columns for the data.

Area Code	@11:11	State	@18:18	County	@26:26	Area Title	@76:
CN010010	|	01	|	001	|	Autauga County, AL	|
PA011000	|	01	|	003	|	Baldwin County, AL	|

4. Click into the data columns and set the titles as follows (the "**|**" columns should not be titled):

- ❑ **Area Code**
- ❑ **State**
- ❑ **County**
- ❑ **Area Title**
- ❑ **Period**
- ❑ **Civilian Labor Force**
- ❑ **Employed**

    ❑   **Unemployed Level**

    ❑   **Unemployed Rate**

5. Click on **Finish** to close the wizard.

6. Manually remove the non-labeled columns (that were the "**|**" columns). Modify the **Period** value to parse the date:

```
Date#(Left(Trim(@77:87), 6), 'MMM-YY') as Period,
```

7. Add a `Where` clause at the end, just before the semi-colon:

```
Where IsNum(Date#(Left(Trim(@77:87), 6), 'MMM-YY'));
```

8. After manually removing the non-labeled columns from the script, your script should look similar to the following code:

```
Temp_Data:
LOAD @1:10 as [Area Code],
     @12:17 as State,
     @19:25 as County,
     @27:75 as [Area Title],
     Date#(Left(Trim(@77:87), 6), 'MMM-YY') as Period,
     @89:100 as [Civilian Labor Force],
     @102:113 as Employed,
     @115:124 as [Unemployed Level],
     @126:n as [Unemployed Rate]
FROM
[laucntycur14.txt]
(fix, codepage is 1252, header is 7 lines)
Where IsNum(Date#(Left(Trim(@77:87), 6), 'MMM-YY'));
```

9. Reload the script.

How to do it...

These steps show you how to use `Peek` and `Previous` to perform calculations against loaded records:

1. Add the following script:

```
LaborData:
Load
   [Area Code],
   State,
   County,
   [Area Title],
```

```
        Period,
        [Civilian Labor Force],
        Employed,
        [Unemployed Level],
        [Unemployed Rate],
        if(Previous([Area Code]) = [Area Code],
          [Unemployed Level]
       -Previous([Unemployed Level]),
            0) As [Rate of Change],
        if(Previous([Area Code]) = [Area Code],
          [Unemployed Level]
       -Previous([Unemployed Level])
       +Peek('Cumulative Change'),
            0) As [Cumulative Change]
      Resident
        Temp_Data
      Order by [Area Code], Period;

      Drop Table Temp_Data;
```

2. Reload the script.
3. Add a table box with all of the fields. Note the values in **Rate of Change** and **Cumulative Change**.

How it works...

The most important thing here is the Order By clause that sorts the data. If the data is sorted by Area Code and Period, we know that if the current Area Code value is not the same as the last one, which we establish using Previous, then we are on the first row for that Area Code and the values should be 0.

We use Previous again to subtract the current unemployment value from the previous one to get a change value.

In the second calculation, we use the same subtraction to get the rate, but add it to the calculation from the previous row to create a cumulative sum. The calculation from the previous row isn't available using Previous, so we use Peek to retrieve it from the memory.

There's more...

Previous expressions can be nested. For example:

```
    Previous(Previous(Previous(FieldName)))
```

Will retrieve the field value from three rows previous to the current row.

Similarly, you can use `Peek` with an offset to get, say, the third-last value:

```
Peek('FieldName', -3, 'TableName')
```

Creating a simple Gantt for a dashboard using Interval Match

There is no native Gantt chart in QlikView. A simple one can be created using a bar chart with bar offset, or a more advanced one can be created by using extension objects (there are some examples of this available online).

In this example, we will use a native QlikView straight table to represent a simple Gantt for use in a dashboard.

Getting ready

Load the following script:

```
Project:
Load * Inline [
ProjectID, ProjectName, StartDate, EndDate
1, First Project, 2013-01-01, 2013-06-30
2, Second Project, 2013-02-01, 2013-07-31
3, Third Project, 2013-03-01, 2013-05-31
4, Fourth Project, 2013-04-01, 2013-08-31
5, Fifth Project, 2013-05-01, 2013-10-31
];

Let vMinDate=Floor(MakeDate(2013));
Let vMaxDate=Floor(MakeDate(2013,10,31));
Let vNumDays=vMaxDate-vMinDate+1;

Calendar:
Load
   TempDate as DateID,
   Date(TempDate) As Date,
   Year(TempDate) As Year,
   Month(TempDate) As Month,
   Date(MonthStart(TempDate), 'YYYY-MM') As YearMonth;
Load
   RecNo()-1+$(vMinDate) As TempDate
AutoGenerate($(vNumDays));
```

```
LinkTable:
IntervalMatch(DateID)
Load
  StartDate, EndDate
Resident Project;
```

How to do it...

Follow these steps to create a simple Gantt for a dashboard:

1. Add a straight table to the layout. Add `ProjectID` and `ProjectName` as dimensions. Add the following expression:

Label	Expression
=Min(YearMonth) & ' - ' & Max(YearMonth)	1

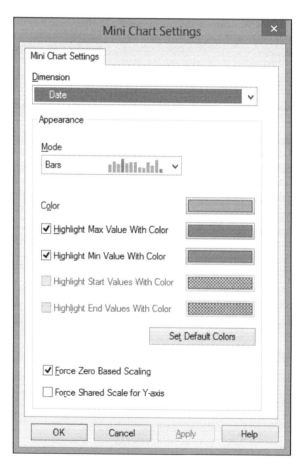

2. Set **Representation** to **Mini Chart**. Click on the **Mini Chart Settings** button. Select **Date** as the dimension and set **Mode** to **Bars**. Click on **OK**.

3. Click on **Finish** to save the chart:

Project Gantt		🖳 XL
ID	ProjectName	2013-01 - 2013-10
1	First Project	
2	Second Project	
3	Third Project	
4	Fourth Project	
5	Fifth Project	

How it works...

By using the `IntervalMatch` function to match the start and end dates of each project to a calendar, we can then use the `Date` field in the mini chart to represent the start and end dates.

The mini chart actually displays a small single vertical bar for each date. Since there is no space between them, it looks like a single horizontal bar. Since the expression is set to `1`, the height of each bar is the same.

See also

▸ The *Matching financial periods to dates* recipe in this chapter

Reading users from Active Directory

Being able to query the Active directory can be very important for a number of reasons. It could be that you just need all the organization unit information. You might also want to read the user data in to integrate with Section Access security.

In this recipe, we will see how to make a simple query to the active directory by using the OLEDB provider for Microsoft Directory Services.

Getting ready

Create a new QlikView document. Set the **Database** drop-down list to **OLEDB** and click on **Connect**.

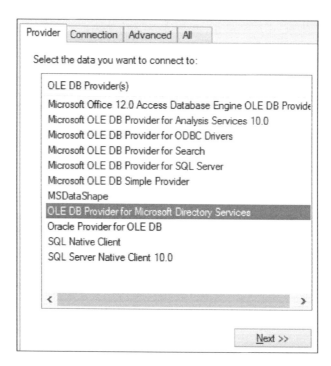

Select **OLEDB Provider for Microsoft Directory Services** and click on **Next**. On the **Connection** tab, select **Use Windows NT Integrated Security** and click on **OK**.

How to do it...

These steps show how to read users from Active Directory:

1. Enter the following script after the database `Connect` statement (modify the `LDAP` URI as appropriate for your domain):

    ```
    Load *,SubField(distinguishedName, ',') As Properties;
    SQL SELECT
      displayName,
    ```

```
        distinguishedName,
        SAMAccountName,
        mail,
        userPrincipalName,
        SN,
        givenName,
        physicalDeliveryOfficeName,
        userAccountControl
   FROM 'LDAP://mydomain.local'
   WHERE objectCategory = 'Person' AND objectClass = 'user';
```

2. Reload the script.

3. Add a table box and add all the fields except properties. Add a second table box and add `displayName` and `Properties`. Note the values.

How it works...

The provider allows us to make these calls against the Active Directory.

The `distinguishedName` field will return the full level of the name; for example:

```
CN=Angela Bloggs,OU=Marketing,OU=Other Users,DC=mydomain,DC=local
```

The `SubField` function, without specifying a third parameter, will split all of these values into multiple rows. So, you will get multiple rows for each user, but QlikView doesn't care about that and handles it perfectly.

Getting a sub-URL using the Table wizard

The table file wizard in QlikView has a lot of functions that aren't for everyday use, but are quite useful to know about, for when you need them.

In this recipe, we are going to look at extracting the data from a website by using the wizard and then extracting sub-URLs from that data.

Getting ready

Create and save a new, blank QlikView document.

How to do it...

These steps show you how to extract a URL from a hyperlink by using the table wizard:

1. Edit the script and click on the **Web Files...** button. Enter `http://www.imdb.com` as the Internet File:

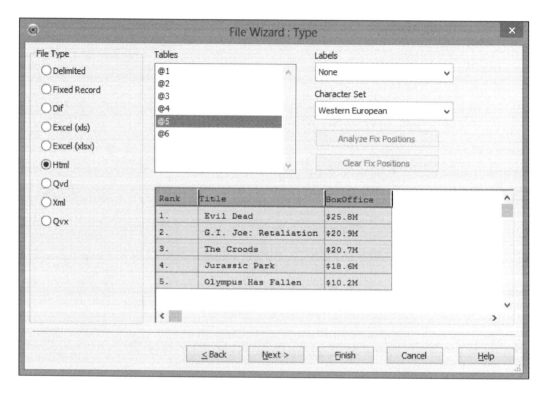

2. Select the table that shows the top five movies. Set **Labels** to **None**. Enter labels for each of the columns. Click on the **Next** button, then **Enable Transformation Step**.

3. Click on the **Column** tab. Click on the **New** button. **Source Column** should be **2** (the column with the movie name in it) and **Target Column** should be **0** (create a new column). Click on the **Cells from these rows...** button. In the **Specify Row Condition** dialog box, select **All Rows** and click on **Add**. Click on **OK**. Click on **OK** to add the new column:

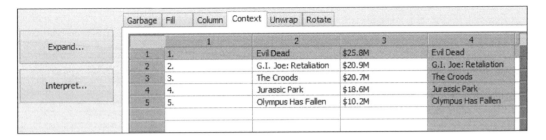

4. Click on the column number for column 4 (the newly added column). Click on the row number for row 1. A grayed intersection should be available and the **Interpret** button should be available. Click on the **Interpret** button:

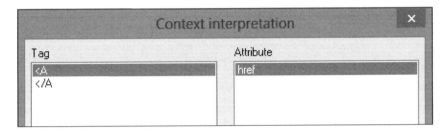

5. Select the **<A** Tag. Select the **href** attribute. Click on **OK**.

6. Click on **Next** on **File Wizard**. Label the columns as appropriate and click on **Finish**. The script should look similar to the following:

```
LOAD @1 as Rank,
    @2 as Title,
    @3 as BoxOffice,
    @4 as URL
FROM
[http://www.imdb.com/]
(html, codepage is 1252, no labels, table is @5, filters(
ColXtr(2, RowCnd(Every), 0),
Interpret(4, '<A', 'href', 1)
));
```

7. Reload the script.

How it works...

The default for the HTML data is to read the text. The `Interpret` function in the wizard allows us to parse out the tag information and gets the values.

There's more...

The file wizard is definitely a tool that you should explore and play with.

Many sites use tables like this, and I have used it for purposes from retrieving exchange rates to grabbing cooking recipes to loading census data.

Using parameters in Dollar Sign Expansion

In the script, we generally use Dollar Sign Expansion to access variable values. However, we can also use them to create macro functions in the script. This is very useful if you need to repeat a function several times.

In this recipe, we are going to extend the mapping function by being able to pass two parameters, and return a different result depending upon which one maps successfully.

Getting ready

Load the following script:

```
Map1:
Mapping Load * Inline [
  map_from, map_to
  A, 1
  B, 2
  C, 3
];

Map2:
Mapping Load * Inline [
  map_from, map_to
  A, 0.1
  B, 0.2
  C, 0.3
];

SET myMacro=Alt(ApplyMap('Map1', $1, Null()), ApplyMap('Map2', $2,
Null()), 0);
```

```
Load
  *
Inline [
  Parm1, Parm2
  A, A
  A, B
  B, A
  C, A
  D, A
  D, B
];
```

How to do it...

These steps show how to use parameters in a dollar sign expansion:

1. Add a table box and add `Parm1` and `Parm2`.

2. Edit the script. Replace the * with the following:

   ```
   *, $(myMacro(Parm1, Parm2)) As Res
   ```

3. Reload and add the `Res` field to the table box.

4. Note the values, especially for `Parm1` of D.

How it works...

The `$1` and `$2` values in the `SET` statement are the parameters and will have their values replaced on each call. In this case, the first `ApplyMap` value will return `Null` if it fails and then the second one will be checked by the `Alt` function.

Removing fields with a wildcard

This particular recipe was inspired by a client of mine who was loading data from a shared set of QVDs. There were a lot of fields in the QVDs that he didn't need and he was wondering if he could; rather than manually pruning the `load` statement, automatically remove fields based on a wild card (all the fields that he wanted removed had the word CUSTOM_ at the beginning).

Unfortunately, we cannot use wildcards in the `Drop Fields` statement. There are a couple of useful functions that we can use to achieve this.

Getting ready

Load the following script:

```
MyTable:
LOAD * INLINE [
F1, F2, F3, F4
1, 2, 3, 4
];

Rename Field F1 to NewField;
Rename Field F3 to NewField2;
```

How to do it...

Use these steps to see how to remove fields with a wildcard:

1. Add the following script:

    ```
    Let i = 1;

    Do While i <= NoOfFields('MyTable')

       Trace Getting Field $(i) From MyTable;

       Let FieldName = FieldName($(i), 'MyTable');

       Trace FieldName = $(FieldName);

       If '$(FieldName)' Like 'F*' Then
         Let Command = 'Drop Field [$(FieldName)];';
         $(Command)
         Trace Command = $(Command);
       Else
         Let Command = '';
         Let i=i+1;
       End If

    Loop
    ```

    Note that you may see syntax highlighting indicating an error in the code.
    There isn't; the parser just can't handle the dollar sign expansion command.

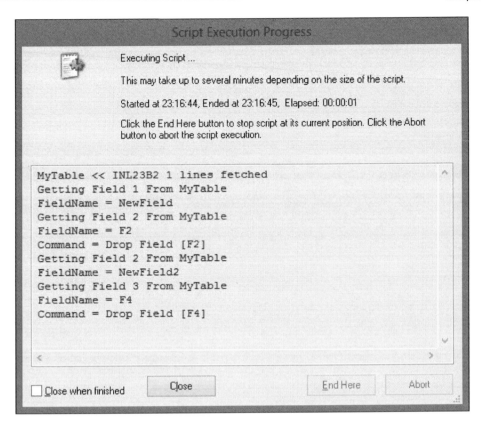

2. Use the **Debug** option in the script editor to reload the script and use the **Step** button to step through each line of code.

3. Note that only two fields are remaining.

How it works...

The `NoOfFields` function will return the number of fields in a named table. We use `FieldName` with the index to return the name of the field, which we can then compare to the wildcard. If it matches, we load a variable with the command to drop that field, then use dollar sign expansion to insert that command into the script.

Note that we don't increase the index after dropping the field; only if we don't drop a field. This is because the field indexes will reset after the drop and the next field along will now occupy that index position.

This is a good example of the technique that dynamically generates, script and then inserts it into the main script by using dollar sign expansion.

If you find it hard to work out what is going in a script, the debug option is a great way of following it.

Handling multiple subfolders in a script

Depending upon the setup that you have to deal with, not all of your source data files may be in one folder. For example, a company may keep transaction files in a separate folder for each year and then one subfolder for each month.

This recipe gives an example of how to use DirList and FileList to retrieve files matching a particular filespec.

Getting ready

Load the following script:

```
Sub GetFiles(vPath)

    // Get a list of files with Q extensions
    For each vFile in FileList('$(vPath)\*.Q*')

        Files:
        Load
          '$(vPath)' as Folder,
          '$(vFile)' as File,
          FileSize('$(vFile)') As FileSize,
          FileTime('$(vFile)') As FileTime
        AutoGenerate(1);

    Next

End Sub

Sub GetSubFolders(vPath)

    For each vDir in DirList('$(vPath)\*')
```

```
Folders:
Load
  '$(vDir)' As Folder
AutoGenerate(1);

Call GetFiles('$(vDir)');
// recurse to get sub folders
Call GetSubFolders('$(vDir)');

  Next

End Sub

Call GetFiles('c:\Program Files\QlikView');
Call GetSubFolders('c:\Program Files\QlikView');
```

How to do it...

These steps show you how to see the results of the folder and files script:

1. Add a table box to the layout and add fields for **Folder, File, FileSize,** and **FileTime**.

2. Edit the properties of the table box. On the **Presentation** tab, select the **File** field and select the **Omit Rows Where Field is NULL** option.

How it works...

Both the `DirList` and `FileList` functions return a list of values that we can use in the `For Each` loop.

By calling the `GetSubFolders` subroutine recursively, we can get down to all the subfolder levels.

10
Improving Performance

In this chapter, we will cover:

- ▶ Reducing the number of distinct values
- ▶ Creating counter fields to avoid Count Distinct
- ▶ Creating flag fields to avoid Sum of If and other inefficient expressions
- ▶ Denormalizing for performance

Introduction

When is application performance tuning necessary? All the time! A QlikView document has several factors that determine how it will perform. Some of these are:

- ▶ The amount of memory on the Server
- ▶ The number of CPU cores available on the Server
- ▶ The amount of data in the document
- ▶ Efficiency of the data model
- ▶ Efficiency of the expressions in charts
- ▶ Number of objects on the layout

As a developer, you may have very little influence on some of these factors. You might have no say in the specification of the server. You may have no influence on the business decision on how many years of data need to be contained in the document. Yet you can very much influence the efficiency of the data model, the efficiency of expressions, and the number of objects on the layout. Even within the constraints of the amount of data required by the business, you can make decisions that will improve the performance.

In this chapter, we will build a large QlikView document and then make adjustments that will make the document more efficient.

Reducing the number of distinct values

QlikView's columnar data storage method is extremely efficient at storing data because it does not store repeating values. Each unique value is only stored once. This means that, in general, a QlikView in-memory data set will always be much smaller than the original data source.

This efficiency is lost, however, when the data is highly distinct. The more distinct the values that exist within the data, the more space that QlikView will need to store it in memory. The worst offenders for this are often ID fields and time stamps, and if we can remove these, then we will make our document more efficient.

Getting ready

Load the following script:

```
// Build a list of city/countries
City_Country:
Load * Inline [
  CityID, City, Country
  1, Boston, USA
  2, New York, USA
  3, Los Angeles, USA
  4, Mexico City, Mexico
  5, Vancouver, Canada
  6, Montreal, Canada
  7, London, UK
  8, Manchester, UK
  9, Berlin, Germany
  10, Paris, France
];

Store City_Country into City_Country.qvd;

Drop Table City_Country;

// Generate suppliers
Supplier:
Load
  RowNo() As SupplierID,
```

```
    'Supplier ' & Num(RowNo(), '(HEX)0') As SupplierName,
    Ceil(Rand() * 10) As CityID
AutoGenerate(15);


Left Join (Supplier)
Load
  CityID,
  City as SupplierCity,
  Country as SupplierCountry
From City_Country.qvd (QVD);


Drop Field CityID From Supplier;


Store Supplier into Supplier.qvd;


Drop Table Supplier;


// Generate some products
Product:
Load
    *,
    Round(CostPrice * (1+Markup), 0.01) As UnitPrice;
Load
  RecNo() As ProductID,
  'Product ' & Num(RecNo(), '(HEX)00') As ProductName,
  Round((Rand() * 0.35 + 0.05), 0.05) As Markup,
  Round(Rand() * 1000, 0.01) As CostPrice,
  Ceil(Rand() * 15) As SupplierID
AutoGenerate(255);


Store Product into Product.qvd;


Drop Table Product;


// Generate some customers
Customer:
Load
  RowNo() As CustomerID,
  'Customer ' & Num(RowNo(), '(HEX)000') As CustomerName,
  Ceil(Rand() * 10) As CityID
AutoGenerate(4095);
```

```
Store Customer into Customer.qvd;

Drop Table Customer;

// Build Calendar
Let vStartDate=Floor(MakeDate(2012));
Let vEndDate=Floor(Today());
let vNumDays=vEndDate-vStartDate+1;

Calendar:
Load
  TempDate as DateID,
  Date(TempDate) As Date,
  Year(TempDate) As Year,
  Month(TempDate) As Month,
  Day(TempDate) As Day,
  WeekDay(TempDate) As WeekDay,
  Week(TempDate) As Week,
  'Q' & Ceil(Month(TempDate)/3) As Quarter,
  Date(MonthStart(TempDate), 'YYYY-MM') As YearMonth,
  Year(TempDate) & '-Q' & Ceil(Month(TempDate)/3)
As YearQuarter,
  WeekYear(TempDate) & '-' & Num(Week(TempDate), '00')
As YearWeek;
Load
  RecNo()-1+$(vStartDate) As TempDate
AutoGenerate($(vNumDays));

Store Calendar into Calendar.qvd;

Drop Table Calendar;

// Load a mapping of product price
Product_Price_Map:
Mapping Load
  ProductID,
  UnitPrice
From Product.qvd (QVD);

// Generate the sales data
Sales:
Load
```

```
  *,
  SalePrice * Quantity * (1-Discount) As Sales;
Load
  *,
  Floor(TransactionDate) As DateID,
  ApplyMap('Product_Price_Map', ProductID, 0) As SalePrice;
Load
  RecNo() As SalesID,
  TimeStamp($(vStartDate)+(Rand()*$(vNumDays)))
As TransactionDate,
  Ceil(Rand() * 255) As ProductID,
  Ceil(Rand() * 4095) As CustomerID,
  Round(Rand() * 0.25, 0.05) As Discount,
  Ceil(Rand() * 100) As Quantity
AutoGenerate(5000000);

Store Sales into Sales.qvd;

Drop Table Sales;
```

Confirm that you have several QVD files in the same folder as QVW.

Note that if you have a small amount of memory available to you (about 500 MB of free memory should be enough for this exercise), you may want to reduce the number of Sales rows generated.

How to do it...

The following demonstrates the effect of reducing the number of distinct values:

1. Create a new QVW file in the same folder as the QVD files and load the following script:

```
Sales:
LOAD SalesID,
     TransactionDate,
     DateID,
     ProductID,
     CustomerID,
     Discount,
     Quantity,
     SalePrice,
     Sales
  FROM
```

```
[Sales.qvd]
(qvd);

Calendar:
LOAD DateID,
     Date,
     Year,
     Month,
     Day,
     WeekDay,
     Week,
     Quarter,
     YearMonth,
     YearQuarter,
     YearWeek
FROM
[Calendar.qvd]
(qvd);

Customer:
LOAD CustomerID,
     CustomerName,
     CityID
FROM
[Customer.qvd]
(qvd);

City_Country:
LOAD CityID,
     City,
     Country
FROM
[City_Country.qvd]
(qvd);

Product:
LOAD ProductID,
       SupplierID,
     ProductName,
     Markup,
     CostPrice,
     UnitPrice
```

```
FROM
[Product.qvd]
(qvd);

Supplier:
LOAD SupplierID,
     SupplierName,
     SupplierCity,
     SupplierCountry
FROM
[Supplier.qvd]
(qvd);
```

2. Reload the document and save it and note the file size (mine is approximately 100 MB).

3. From the **Settings** menu, select **Document Properties**. Select the **Tables** tab and then select the **Sales** table as follows:

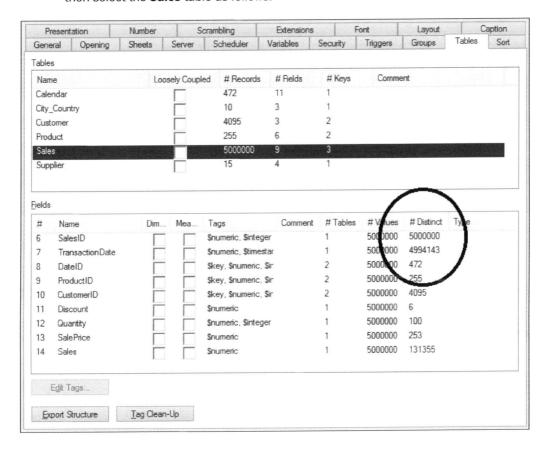

Presentation		Number		Scrambling		Extensions		Font		Layout		Caption	
General	Opening	Sheets	Server	Scheduler	Variables	Security	Triggers	Groups	Tables	Sort

Tables

Name	Loosely Coupled	# Records	# Fields	# Keys	Comment
Calendar		472	11	1	
City_Country		10	3	1	
Customer		4095	3	2	
Product		255	6	2	
Sales		5000000	9	3	
Supplier		15	4	1	

Fields

#	Name	Dim...	Mea...	Tags	Comment	# Tables	# Values	# Distinct	Type
6	SalesID			$numeric, $integer		1	5000000	5000000	
7	TransactionDate			$numeric, $timestam		1	5000000	4994143	
8	DateID			$key, $numeric, $in		2	5000000	472	
9	ProductID			$key, $numeric, $in		2	5000000	255	
10	CustomerID			$key, $numeric, $in		2	5000000	4095	
11	Discount			$numeric		1	5000000	6	
12	Quantity			$numeric, $integer		1	5000000	100	
13	SalePrice			$numeric		1	5000000	253	
14	Sales			$numeric		1	5000000	131355	

Edit Tags...

Export Structure   Tag Clean-Up

4. Note that the **SalesID** field and the **TransactionDate** field have a large number of **Distinct** values. However, the **SalesID** field is not used for association in this application and, because the date is already included in the **DateID** field, we really don't need the time stamp.

5. Modify the script to load the sales table as follows:

```
Sales:
LOAD //SalesID,
     Hour(TransactionDate) As TransHour,
     DateID,
     ProductID,
     CustomerID,
     Discount,
     Quantity,
     SalePrice,
     Sales
FROM
[Sales.qvd]
(qvd);
```

6. Reload the document and note the file size (mine is down to approximately 45MB). The file should have reduce by about half from the original.

How it works...

By removing the highly unique fields, we have made a huge difference to the size of the document.

Transaction IDs are almost never needed in a document.

We have changed the time stamp from a field that had almost 5,000,000 unique values to a field that has only 24 unique values (hours), and still have the required business functionality. In fact, the business is probably better served by a more efficient document.

There's more...

Always look out for the **# Distinct** field in the **Tables** tab of **Document Properties**. If it is large relative to the number of rows, think about whether that field is needed at all, or what can be done to reduce the uniqueness.

See also

▸ Consolidating a date-time value into quarter hourly segments.

Creating counter fields to avoid Count Distinct

Using a Count function is a very common use case in any type of reporting. However, it is also a very laborious calculation, requiring many more CPU cycles than, say, a Sum function. This is because a function like Sum is actually a very low-level function, operating almost at the CPU level, whereas a function like Count is more high-level, operating at the application code level. On a multi-threaded system (which means almost all systems nowadays), the Sum function will run across all cores whereas the Count function will only calculate on one thread.

If we can avoid Count functions, especially a Count function with a Distinct clause, then we will have a more efficient application.

Getting ready

Generate QVDs created in the *Reducing the number of distinct values* recipe.

How to do it...

These steps show you how to create counter fields to avoid Count Distinct:

1. Create a new QlikView file in the same folder as the QVDs. Load the following script:

```
LOAD SalesID,
     TransactionDate,
     ProductID,
     CustomerID,
     Discount,
     Quantity,
     DateID,
     SalePrice,
     Sales
FROM
[Sales.qvd]
(qvd);
```

2. Reload and save the QVW file. Note the file size.

3. Modify the script as follows:

```
LOAD //SalesID,
     1 as SalesTransCounter,
```

```
                TransactionDate,
                ProductID,
                CustomerID,
                Discount,
                Quantity,
                DateID,
                SalePrice,
                Sales
    FROM
    [Sales.qvd]
    (qvd);
```

4. Reload and save the QVW file. Note that the file size has not necessarily decreased (and may have increased!).

5. Add a chart with **ProductID** as the dimension. Add the following expression:

    `Sum(SalesTransCounter)`

6. The total (with no selections) should add to 5,000,000.

How it works...

We have removed the ID value that we might have used as a `Count` function on and replaced it with a single value—1—that will be summed instead. This function will calculate multiple times faster than the `Count` function.

Even though we have got rid of a very unique value, QlikView still needs to store keys to associate the single—1—value to the other values in the table.

There's more...

The more that this `Count` function might be used in a QlikView application, the more that you should consider that it should be replaced. By targeting more frequently used expressions in your application, you will really improve the efficiency.

Note that I included the new **SalesTransCounter** field in the load script of the final QVW when loading from the QVD file. Normally this would not happen here as it removes the optimized load from QVD file. Instead, it would normally happen in the QVD generation script.

See also

▶ The *Reducing the number of distinct values* recipe in this chapter.

Creating flag fields to avoid Sum of If and other inefficient expressions

The more efficient our expressions are, the more efficient the whole document will be – especially where those expressions are used frequently.

Many times, with a more complex expression, just thinking about what is happening might lead you to come up with a flag field that could be precalculated in the script.

Calculation of a flag field does add extra time to the load script. It can also increase the size of the data set. But they are a lot quicker on the front-end, and that makes the document more efficient for users.

Getting ready

Generate QVDs created in the *Reducing the number of distinct values* recipe.

How to do it...

Follow these steps to create flag fields to avoid Sum of If expression and other inefficient expressions:

1. Create a new QVW file in the same folder as QVDs and load the following script:

    ```
    Calendar:
    LOAD DateID,
         Date,
         If(Year2Date(Date, 0, 1, Today()), 1, 0) As YTDFlag,
         Year,
         Month,
         Day,
         WeekDay,
         Week,
         Quarter,
         YearMonth,
         YearQuarter,
         YearWeek
    FROM
    [Calendar.qvd]
    (qvd);

    Sales:
    ```

```
LOAD //SalesID,
      1 as SalesTransCounter,
      TransactionDate,
      ProductID,
      CustomerID,
      Discount,
      Quantity,
      DateID,
      If(Year2Date(DateID, 0, 1, Today()), 1, 0) As YTDFlag2,
      SalePrice,
      Sales
FROM
[Sales.qvd]
(qvd);
```

2. Reload the script. Add a **Straight Table** type with no dimension, and add the following expression:

   ```
   Sum(If(Year2Date(Date, 0, 1, Today()), Sales, 0))
   ```

3. Add a second **Straight Table** again with no dimension. Add the following expression:

   ```
   Sum({<YTDFlag={1}>} Sales)
   ```

4. Add a third **Straight Table**, and once again with no dimension. Add the following expression:

   ```
   Sum({<YTDFlag2={1}>} Sales)
   ```

5. Save and close the document and QlikView. After a moment, restart QlikView and then reopen the document.

6. From the **Settings** menu, select **Document Properties**. Click on the **Sheets** tab and look at the details for the charts in the lower panel:

SheetID	ObjectID	Type	Caption	ShowMode	CalcTime	Layer	Memory	Le
SH01	CH02	Straight Table	Sum of If	Normal	749	0	2 KB	
SH01	CH03	Straight Table	Flag Calculation	Normal	187	0	2 KB	
SH01	CH04	Straight Table	Flag Calculation 2	Normal	156	0	2 KB	

7. Compare the **CalcTime** value for each chart and note that the calculation with the flag field, as it is significantly quicker than the "Sum of If" statement. The second flag field has a slight improvement over the first.

How it works...

We have pushed the processing of the If statement into the script and created a simple numeric field that we can use in a Set syntax. The Set syntax means that only the matching values get included in the Sum function whereas with a Sum of If expression, all the values—whether zero or not—will be included in the Sum function. This calculation may be performed many times on the front-end so that it makes sense to push the calculation into the script.

The second flag field is "co-located" in the same table as the Sales figure and, as such, will have a direct binary key relationship. The first one is in the Calendar table, so there is an extra layer of association between them, which is why there is a small increase in its performance.

There's more...

We had to close and reopen QlikView to clear the cache so as to have the charts recalculate. Otherwise, the charts would calculate from the cache and the **CalcTime** value would be a lot lower.

The second flag field does give us a performance improvement over the first, and this can be significant. The trade-off is that there may be a larger data size.

Note that the YTD flags here are created in the load script of the final QVW when loading from the QVD file. Normally this would not happen here as it removes the optimized load from QVD. Instead, it would normally happen in the QVD generation script.

Here are some other interesting expressions that you might like to test:

```
Sum(if(YTDFlag=1,Sales,0))
```

and

```
Sum(Sales*YTDFlag)
```

See also

► The *Reducing the number of distinct values* recipe in this chapter
► The *Creating counter fields to avoid Count Distinct* recipe in this chapter

Denormalizing for performance

Good transactional database design suggests that data tables should be normalized, at least to third normal form. But this is not necessarily the most efficient for QlikView.

In a QlikView data model, the more association links between two fields, the longer it will take to calculate the result of one versus the other.

By that logic, it might make sense to consider that a single table model is the most efficient in QlikView. But that is not necessarily the case either.

Getting ready

Generate QVDs created in the *Reducing the number of distinct values* recipe.

How to do it...

These steps demonstrate how to denormalize for performance:

1. Create a new QVW file in the same folder as QVDs and load the following script:

    ```
    Sales:
    LOAD //SalesID,
          Hour(TransactionDate) As TransHour,
          DateID,
          ProductID,
          CustomerID,
          Discount,
          Quantity,
          SalePrice,
          Sales
    FROM
    [Sales.qvd]
    (qvd);

    Calendar:
    LOAD DateID,
         Date,
         Year,
         Month,
         Day,
         WeekDay,
         Week,
    ```

```
          Quarter,
          YearMonth,
          YearQuarter,
          YearWeek
FROM
[Calendar.qvd]
(qvd);

Customer:
LOAD CustomerID,
     CustomerName,
     CityID
FROM
[Customer.qvd]
(qvd);

City_Country:
LOAD CityID,
     City,
     Country
FROM
[City_Country.qvd]
(qvd);

Product:
LOAD ProductID,
     SupplierID,
     ProductName,
     Markup,
     CostPrice,
     UnitPrice
FROM
[Product.qvd]
(qvd);

Supplier:
LOAD SupplierID,
     SupplierName,
     SupplierCity,
     SupplierCountry
FROM
[Supplier.qvd]
(qvd);
```

2. Reload and save the document. Note the file size.

3. Open the Table Viewer and note the table structure as shown:

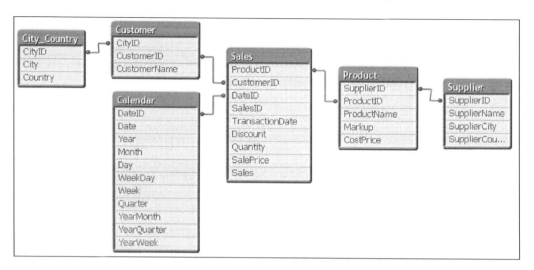

4. Save the document with a new name and edit the script as follows:

```
Sales:
LOAD //SalesID,
     Hour(TransactionDate) As TransHour,
     DateID,
     ProductID,
     CustomerID,
     Discount,
     Quantity,
     SalePrice,
     Sales
FROM
[Sales.qvd]
(qvd);

Calendar:
Left Join (Sales)
LOAD DateID,
     Date,
     Year,
     Month,
     Day,
```

```
            WeekDay,
            Week,
            Quarter,
            YearMonth,
            YearQuarter,
            YearWeek
FROM
[Calendar.qvd]
(qvd);

Customer:
Left Join (Sales)
LOAD CustomerID,
        CustomerName,
        CityID
FROM
[Customer.qvd]
(qvd);

City_Country:
Left Join (Sales)
LOAD CityID,
        City,
        Country
FROM
[City_Country.qvd]
(qvd);

Product:
Left Join (Sales)
LOAD ProductID,
        SupplierID,
        ProductName,
        Markup,
        CostPrice,
        UnitPrice
FROM
[Product.qvd]
(qvd);

Supplier:
Left Join (Sales)
```

```
LOAD SupplierID,
     SupplierName,
     SupplierCity,
     SupplierCountry
FROM
[Supplier.qvd]
(qvd);

Drop Fields DateID, CustomerID, CityID, ProductID, SupplierID;
```

5. Reload the script. Open the Table Viewer and note that this is now only one table. Save the document and note the size of the file. It is larger than the previous.

6. Save the document with another new name. Edit the script and comment out the join statement for the `Calendar` and the `Product` table.

7. Reload and save the document. Note that the size is lower than the first.

How it works...

By joining all the tables into the main fact table, we can create a single table structure which should be quite efficient.

There's more...

As a general principal, the lesser number of "hops" between tables the better. However, when we join a dimension table with several fields into a fact table, we are increasing the number of keys necessary for QlikView to associate the data, thus increasing the size of the document.

A "Kimball" style star schema is probably the best design approach to a QlikView data set, but QlikView is quite flexible in this regard.

One thing to watch out for when joining dimension tables into fact tables is that the dimension key must be unique, otherwise you will generate duplicates in your fact table.

Note that the **TransHour** field here is created in the load script of the final QVW when loading from the QVD file. Normally this would not happen here as it removes the optimized load from QVD. Instead, it would normally happen in the QVD generation script.

See also

▸ The *Reducing the number of distinct values* recipe in this chapter

11
Security

In this chapter, we will cover:

- ▸ Section Access gotchas
- ▸ Blocking user access to a field using OMIT
- ▸ Making all values available to Admins

Introduction

Security in QlikView is both simple and powerful.

It is as simple as connecting a user to the data. By connecting the user to the data, we restrict access to the document and we can also restrict the user to only view the data that they are connected to.

While it is a pretty simple setup, there are a few things that are useful to know to ease the implementation.

In the following exercises, we will use the **USERID** field to allow us to easily test different users. This is a QlikView user, which will be used less in live implementations than the NTNAME, which links to either Windows usernames or a username passed by another authentication mechanism.

Section Access gotchas

When setting up Section Access, there are a few common things that can lead to failure. A failure in Section Access can be more upsetting when you find that you can no longer open your QlikView document.

In this recipe, we will create a few of these errors and show how to resolve them.

Getting ready

Load the following script:

```
//Section Access;
Access:
LOAD * INLINE [
    ACCESS, USERID, PASSWORD, Link
    ADMIN, admin, admin, *
    USER, user1, user1, US
    USER, user2, user2, UK
    USER, user3, user3, Fr
];

Section Application;

Sales:
Load * Inline [
    Link, Country, Sales
    US, USA, 1000
    UK, United Kingdom, 800
    Fr, France, 750
    De, Germany, 940
];
```

Save this document as `Security1.qvw` and reload.

How to do it...

1. Add the **USERID** and **Country** fields to the layout:

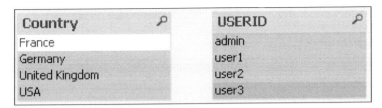

2. Confirm that each user is associated with the values that are expected (the admin user will not be associated with any country – this is expected).

3. Save the document as `Security2.qvw`. Edit the script and uncomment the Section Access statement. Reload the document, and the **USERID** field will become unavailable.

4. From the **Settings** menu, select **Document Properties** and click on the **Opening** tab. Turn on the **Initial Data Reduction Based on Section Access** option. Make sure that **Strict Exclusion** is also selected.

5. Save and close the document.

6. From the **Settings** menu, select **User Preferences**. Make sure that the **Remember Login Credentials Until QlikView Exits** option is unchecked and click on **OK**.

7. Reopen the `Security2.qvw` file. Try logging in as any of the users (`user1`/`user2`/ `user3`). It is expected that the users should only see one country. However, each user can still see several of them.

8. Close the document and then reopen it and log in as admin. Edit the script and, in the `Access` table, change the **Link** field name from **Link** to **LINK**. Repeat for the **Link** field in the `Sales` table.

9. Reload and save the document. Close and reopen the document. Log in as `user1`. Only **USA** should be listed.

10. Close the document and reopen. Try logging in as `user3`. Now the access is denied to the document!

11. Open the document and log in as admin. Edit the script. Change the **Link** field value, in both `Access` and `Sales` table, from **Fr** to **FR**. Reload, save, and close the document.

12. Reopen the document and you should now be able to login as `user3` and only see **France**.

13. Close, reopen, and log in as admin. Notice that you can see several countries but **Germany** is not visible. Reload the document, and **Germany** is now visible again. However, if you save and close, when you reopen and log in as admin again, **Germany** will be gone.

14. Edit the script and add a new line to the `Access` table:

```
Access:
LOAD * INLINE [
    ACCESS, USERID, PASSWORD, LINK
    ADMIN, admin, admin, *
    USER, user1, user1, US
    USER, user2, user2, UK
    USER, user3, user3, FR
    USER, user1, user1, DE
];
```

15. Edit the **Link** value in the `Sales` table from **De** to **DE**. Reload the document, save and close. Now when we reopen and log in as admin, we can see all the countries.

How it works...

There are three "gotcha's" here.

First, we need to remember that any field that is involved with the Section Access tables must be spelled in all capital letters. If we use a mixed case, even though that is valid in QlikView, it does not work.

Secondly, any value that is used in the **Link** field that has letters, must also use capital letters. Mixed case will not work.

Lastly, and this is usually a problem for Admin/Manager users who want to see all of the data, if all of the data is not connected to the section access table, the unconnected data will be removed by the reduction process, even for * connected users. The star is a wildcard that allows the user to be connected to all of the data but it is not considered for the reduction.

There's more...

The reason that we did a **Save As** dialog at the beginning and saved the file as `Security2.qvw` was just-in-case, if there was a problem along the way, we can potentially be locked out of our QlikView document and lose our work!

When a user logs in, the reduction process actually removes the unassociated data from memory. If you saved the document then, it will save with only that user's linked data (which is why the **Save As** dialog will appear if you try).

Loading your data with the Section Access statement commented out can be a useful way of checking your security by being able to select a user and see what they are connected to.

Because of the restriction on the **link** field, which needs to contain capital letter values if letters are used, I would often recommend using numeric values for this link.

See also

▸ The *Blocking user access to a field using OMIT recipe in this chapter*

▸ The *Making All values available to Admins and Managers recipe in this chapter*

Blocking user access to a field using OMIT

It can sometimes happen that some fields in a document should not be seen by some users while being available to others. A classic case might be an HR document, where some users can see the list of employees but might not be able to see the `Salary` field.

We do this by associating the users with a field called `OMIT`. Now, this is QlikView, so it doesn't have to be a 1:1 association, and users can be associated with multiple `OMIT` values.

Getting ready

Load the following script:

```
Section Access;
Access:
LOAD * INLINE [
    ACCESS, USERID, PASSWORD, OMITGROUP
    ADMIN, admin, admin,
    USER, user1, user1,
    USER, user2, user2, SALARYONLY
    USER, user3, user3, SALARYANDABSENCE
    USER, user4, user4, ABSENCEONLY
];

OmitGroups:
LOAD * INLINE [
    OMITGROUP, OMIT
    SALARYONLY, Salary
    SALARYANDABSENCE, Salary
    SALARYANDABSENCE, Absence
    ABSENCEONLY, Absence
];
```

```
Section Application;

//Employees:
LOAD * INLINE [
    EmpID, Name, Salary, Absence
    1, Joe Bloggs, 50000, 3
    2, Jane Doe, 45000, 5
    3, Fred Frank, 30000, 0
    4, Jeri Jublek, 19000, 12
];
```

How to do it...

1. Add fields for **Name**, **Salary**, and **Absence** onto the layout. Save the document and close it.

2. From the **Settings** menu, select **User Preferences...**. Make sure that the **Remember Login Credentials Until QlikView Exits** option is unchecked and click on **OK**.

3. Reopen the document and log in as `Admin`. Confirm that all three fields are still visible and close the document.

4. Reopen the document and log in as `user1`. The three fields should still be visible. Close the document.

Name	(unav...	Absence
Fred Frank		0
Jane Doe		3
Jeri Jublek		5
Joe Bloggs		12

5. Reopen the document and log in as `user2`. The **Name** and **Absence** fields should be visible as normal. The **Salary** field is visible but **(unavailable)** and no data is visible. It is as if the field does not exist. In fact, it doesn't, it has been dropped when the user logged in. Close the document

6. Reopen the document and log in as `user3`. Only the **Name** field is available. Close the document.

7. Finally, reopen and log in as `user4`. The **Absence** field is unavailable.

How it works...

If a user is associated with any value in the OMIT field, that field name is dropped from memory when the user logs in.

`Admin` and `user1` are not linked to any `OMIT` values so they still see all of the fields.

There's more...

Because the field is actually dropped from memory, if you saved the document after logging in as one of the restricted users, the document would save without that field. This is why the **Save As** dialog will appear if you try to save it.

See also

▸ The *Section Access gotchas* recipe in this chapter

Making all values available to Admins and Managers

If all of the data is not connected to the section access table, the unconnected data will be removed by the reduction process – even for * connected users. The Star is a wildcard that allows the user to be connected to all of the data, but it is not considered for the reduction.

This is not so much of a problem if the security model is fairly static. But if the model is dynamic, then we need to be able to make sure that a user who needs to see all of the data can see it.

Getting ready

Load the following script:

```
Section Access;
Access:
LOAD * INLINE [
    ACCESS, USERID, PASSWORD, LINK
    ADMIN, admin, admin, *
    USER, manager1, manager1, ALL
    USER, user1, user1, US
    USER, user2, user2, UK
    USER, user3, user3, FR
];

Section Application;
```

```
Sales:
Load * Inline [
      CountryCode, Country, Sales
      US, USA, 1000
      UK, United Kingdom, 800
      FR, France, 750
      DE, Germany, 940
];

LinkTable:
Load Distinct
   Upper(CountryCode) as LINK,
   CountryCode
Resident
   Sales;

Load Distinct
   'ALL' as LINK,
   CountryCode
Resident
   Sales;
```

How to do it...

1. Add a Table Box to the layout and add the **LINK** and **CountryCode** fields to it:

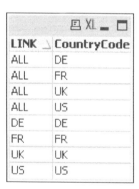

LINK	CountryCode
ALL	DE
ALL	FR
ALL	UK
ALL	US
DE	DE
FR	FR
UK	UK
US	US

2. Note that All of the country codes are linked to the **ALL** value, as well as their own distinct values.

3. Save the document and close it. Reopen and log in as `admin`:

4. Note that the distinct link for **DE** is missing. However, the admin can still see **Germany**.

5. Close the document. Reopen and log in as `manager1`:

6. Note that only the **ALL** link values are listed as these are the only ones that `manager1` is linked to.

How it works...

This is actually beautifully simple. By deriving the **ALL** association from the actual data, `manager1` can see all of the data. As a side effect, the `admin` user can also see all of the data because the `admin` user will also see the **ALL** link.

There's more...

By having just one user linked to the **ALL** value, all users with * associations will also be linked to all of the data.

See also

▶ The *Section Access gotchas* recipe in this chapter

Index

Symbols

 # function 184

A

Above function 191
Active Directory
  users, reading from 227-229
Admins
  values, making available to 263-265
Advanced styling mode 68
AGGR
  used, for calculating maximum value
        percentage 103-105
  using, to resolve Sums of Rows
        issue 106-108
AllowMacroFunctionInExpressions option
  151
alternate states
  using, in Set Analysis 85-90
Alt function 62, 180, 181, 184, 202
AND mode
  using, in listboxes 207-210

B

bar chart
  about 8
  creating, in straight table 31-33
  creating, steps 9
  custom pop-up labels, creating 8-11
  secondary dimension, creating 40-43
box plot chart
  creating, for simple data set 13-18
  creating, wizard used 19-23

budget
  creating, for store 157-159

C

calculations
  null, handling 180, 181
cell
  custom formatting, design menus used 77-80
charts
  about 8
  bar chart 8
  box plot chart 13
  creating, macro used 146-148
  line chart 38
  modified bullet chart 28
  pie chart 55
  Redmond Aged Debt Profile chart 33-35
  scatter chart 52
  Stephen Few bullet chart 23
  VBS functions, using 149-151
  waterfall chart 35
chr function 12
COALESCE function 180
colormix
  used, for creating colored Treemaps 117-120
color scheme
  default gray color scheme, modifying 71-73
  default green color scheme, modifying 71-73
  default selection color scheme,
        changing 69, 70
  default white color scheme, modifying 71-73
containers
  using, as alternative to Multiboxes 75-77
control chart
  creating, Moving Range chart used 131, 132

mR. *See* **Moving Range chart**

Multiboxes
  containers, using as alternative to 75-77

multiple subfolders
  handling, in script 236, 237

N

NoOfFields function 235

null
  handling, in calculations 180, 181
  handling, in numeric fields 180, 181

numbers
  text, parsing to 183, 184

numeric fields
  null, handling 180, 181

O

OMIT
  used, for blocking user access to
    field 261-263

Only() function 189

Override Document Settings option 195

P

parallel coordinates
  about 47
  brushing 47-52

parameters
  using, in dollar sign expansion 232, 233

partial reload
  in script, handling 219, 220

PDF
  reports printing, PDFCreator used 142-145

PDFCreator
  used, for printing reports to PDF 142-145

Peek
  about 221
  data, loading 221-223
  using, to calculate against loaded
    records 223, 224

performance
  denormalizing for 252-256

period name sorting
  handling, Dual used 181, 182

pie chart
  dynamic Part-to-Whole pie chart, creating
    113-117
  labeling, to replace legend 187-189
  labels, staggering 55-57

pivot table
  top 3 values, displaying 124-126

positive numbers
  returning, RangeMax used 110-112

Presentation tab 25

Previous
  about 221, 222
  data, loading 221-223
  using, to calculate against loaded records
    223, 224

Q

QlikView
  aggregations 99
  coding 133
  data, exporting to Word report 134, 140, 142
  data modeling 153
  default layout option, changing 66-69
  default selection color scheme,
    changing 69, 70
  dynamic ad hoc analysis, creating 58, 60-63
  extensions 163, 164
  functions 179
  Key table, creating 157-161
  layout 65
  Link table, creating 157-161
  performance, improving 239
  script 198
  security 257

QlikView Server
  gray color scheme, modifying 74
  green color scheme, modifying 74
  white color scheme, modifying 74

quarter hour segments
  date-time value, consolidating into 192-194

QVD storing
  subroutine used 202, 203

R

range
  highest value, calculating 189-191
  lowest value, calculating 189-191
RangeMax function
  about 112
  using, to return positive numbers 110-112
RangeSum
  using, to calculate rolling totals 121, 122
Redmond Aged Debt Profile chart
  creating 33, 34
reports
  printing to PDF, PDFCreator used 142, 145
Representation property 32
results
  values excluding, Set operators used 91-93
rolling totals
  calculating, RangeSum used 121, 122
RowNo() function 191

S

scatter chart
  redundant encoding, using 52-55
script
  flags, creating 198-200
  multiple subfolders, handling 236, 237
  partial reload, handling 219, 220
Section Access
  about 258, 259
  gotchas 260
SelectRow function 174
Set Analysis
  alternate states, using 85-90
  dollar expansion, using 82-85
  using, with Date Island 93-96
Set operators
  used, for excluding values from results 91-93
Sets
  used, for avoiding Key tables 96-98
Show Caption option 27
Show Grid option 50
Show Legend option 41, 49
simple data set
  box plot chart, creating 13-18

Simple mode 69
sort order
  default sort order, setting 215
Standard Deviation
  used, for creating Statistical Control
    Chart 126-128
Static Max option 50
Static Max setting 27
Statistical Control Chart
  creating, Standard Deviation used 126-128
Stephen Few bullet chart
  about 23
  creating 23-27
  working 27
StockStore field 98
straight table
  bar chart, creating 31, 32
  modified bullet chart, creating 28-30
SubField function 229
subfolders
  multiple subfolders in script,
    handling 236, 237
subroutine
  used, for dropping table 203, 204
  used, for QVD storing 202
  used, for storing QVD 203, 204
sub-URL
  getting, TableWizard used 229-231
Sum (FactValue * Flag) function 187
Sum function 247
Sum of If expression
  avoiding, flag fields created for 249-251
Sums of Rows issue
  resolving, AGGR used 106-108

T

table, dropping
  subroutine used 203
Table wizard
  used, for getting sub-URL 229-232
text
  parsing, to dates 183, 184
  parsing, to numbers 183, 184
TOTAL
  about 100

used, for calculating subtotal
percentage 101, 102
used, for calculating total
percentage 101, 102

Trace
about 205
using 205-207

Treemaps
colored Treemaps creating, colormix used
117-120

U

user
field access blocking, OMIT used 261-263
UserPreferences object 73
users
reading, from Active Directory 227-229

V

values
distinct values number, reducing 240,
243-246
excluding from results, Set operators
used 91-93
making, available to Admins 263-265
making, available to Managers 263-265
Values on Data Points option 189
variable width lines
line chart, creating with 44-46
VBS functions
using, in charts 149-151

W

waterfall chart
creating 35-37
white color scheme
default white color scheme, changing 71-73
on QlikView Server, modifying 74
wildcard
fields, removing with 233-236
wizard
used, for box plot chart creating 19-23
Word report
data, exporting to 134, 140-142

X

X-Axis 8
XmR Chart 132

Y

Y-Axis 8
Year To Date function
dynamic calculation 184-187

Thank you for buying
QlikView for Developers Cookbook

About Packt Publishing

Packt, pronounced 'packed', published its first book "*Mastering phpMyAdmin for Effective MySQL Management*" in April 2004 and subsequently continued to specialize in publishing highly focused books on specific technologies and solutions.

Our books and publications share the experiences of your fellow IT professionals in adapting and customizing today's systems, applications, and frameworks. Our solution-based books give you the knowledge and power to customize the software and technologies you're using to get the job done. Packt books are more specific and less general than the IT books you have seen in the past. Our unique business model allows us to bring you more focused information, giving you more of what you need to know, and less of what you don't.

Packt is a modern, yet unique publishing company, which focuses on producing quality, cutting-edge books for communities of developers, administrators, and newbies alike. For more information, please visit our website: www.PacktPub.com.

About Packt Enterprise

In 2010, Packt launched two new brands, Packt Enterprise and Packt Open Source, in order to continue its focus on specialization. This book is part of the Packt Enterprise brand, home to books published on enterprise software – software created by major vendors, including (but not limited to) IBM, Microsoft and Oracle, often for use in other corporations. Its titles will offer information relevant to a range of users of this software, including administrators, developers, architects, and end users.

Writing for Packt

We welcome all inquiries from people who are interested in authoring. Book proposals should be sent to author@packtpub.com. If your book idea is still at an early stage and you would like to discuss it first before writing a formal book proposal, contact us; one of our commissioning editors will get in touch with you.

We're not just looking for published authors; if you have strong technical skills but no writing experience, our experienced editors can help you develop a writing career, or simply get some additional reward for your expertise.

QlikView 11 for Developers

ISBN: 978-1-849686-06-8   Paperback: 534 pages

Develop Business Intelligence applications with QlikView 11

1. Learn to build applications for Business Intelligence while following a practical case – HighCloud Airlines. Each chapter develops parts of the application and it evolves throughout the book along with your own QlikView skills.

2. The code bundle for each chapter can be accessed on your local machine without having to purchase a QlikView license.

3. The hands-on approach allows you to build a QlikView application that integrates real data from several different sources and presents it in dashboards, analyses and reports.

Oracle Business Intelligence Enterprise Edition 11*g*: A Hands-On Tutorial

ISBN: 978-1-849685-66-5   Paperback: 620 pages

Leverage the latest Fusion Middleware Business Intelligence offering with this action-packed implementation guide

1. Get to grips with the OBIEE 11g suite for analyzing and reporting on your business data

2. Immerse yourself in BI upgrading techniques, using Agents and the Action Framework and much more in this book and e-book

3. A practical, from the coalface tutorial, bursting with step by step instructions and real world case studies to help you implement the suite's powerful analytic capabilities

Please check **www.PacktPub.com** for information on our titles

Made in the USA
Lexington, KY
30 August 2014